PRAISE FOR A SURRE

If I could handpick the perfect person to ... an abortion, it would be my friend Pat L... istic and filled with hope. As a woman who has experienced the depths of emotion an abortion brings, I am so thankful for the *Surrendering the Secret* Bible study and for Pat's new book, *A Surrendered Life*.

Lysa TerKeurst
New York Times Bestselling Author
President, Proverbs 31 Ministries

I have personally heard many stories from people whose lives have been transformed by *Surrendering the Secret*. You will be blessed, too, by *A Surrendered Life*. Having known Pat Layton for years, her compassion, wisdom and inspirational testimony will fill you with hope. *A Surrendered Life* will help you find freedom from the heartache of abortion.

Craig Altman
Lead Pastor, Grace Family Church Tampa, Florida

A Surrendered Life is more than a self-help book! This useful resource written from the heart of Pat Layton, an authentic woman who herself lives a surrendered life, ushers the way for us to gracefully embrace Jesus as the healer who sets the captive free to live the life He intends where we are restored, redeemed and *free indeed*!

Vicky Botsford McCarter
President, LifeSteward Ministries

Pat Layton has spent a lifetime on the front lines helping women find help, hope and a truth that "sets you free." *A Surrendered Life* will help women discover that the surrendered life is the path to their future happiness and wholeness as an individual, in their marriage and for their family.

Pam Farrel
International Speaker
Author of more than 30 books, including *10 Best Decisions a Woman Can Make*
   and the bestselling *Men Are Like Waffles, Women Are Like Spaghetti*

A Surrendered Life is a must-read for those who have surrendered the secret of abortion. This is the book that will inform and inspire you on your journey forward. Nothing encourages quite like the stories of those on the same journey. Read and experience hope.

Dr. Johnny Hunt
Pastor, First Baptist Church Woodstock

A Surrendered Life breaks open the secret that causes so many women and men to suffer. It is a secret that we allow Satan to control. . . and he will continue to take control until we truly surrender that secret to Christ and allow Him to use our past for His glory. Our stories need to be told. I believe this book will inspire the confidence we need to share those stories and find healing in the power of Christ.

Abby Johnson
Author, *Unplanned*

Several years ago Pat Layton and her ministry came to the attention of the women's ministry team at LifeWay. We knew that a vast sea of hurt spread across our land because of abortion, but we had few practical ideas how to minister to that hurt. Partnering with the *Surrendering the Secret* Bible study has provided an opportunity to touch and heal that pain. Thank you, Pat, and those who have shared your ministry, for your transparency, faithfulness, hard work and sacrificial service. My prayer is that *A Surrendered Life* will provide additional ministry to women and men who have been impacted by the heartbreaking choice of abortion.

Dale McCleskey
Editor, LifeWay Christian Resources

A Surrendered Life is a key to unlocking the secret places of millions of women's hearts hurting from abortion. The waters of healing tears need to overflow these secret places, unlocking an army of women ready to do justice and be a witness. Healing comes from confession and surrender.

Allan E. Parker
President, The Justice Foundation

Pat Layton's book is a must-read, providing insight into the journey of healing the wounds of a post-abortive woman. She captivates the hearts of many men and women through her own transparency, testimony and life experiences. Her love is felt with every turn of the page.

Shari Rigby
National Speaker
Actress, *October Baby*

A Surrendered Life is a must-read for anyone who has endured an abortion or loves someone who has. Filled with personal transparency and biblical truth, these pages take the reader on a journey toward freedom where there is hope for real healing. Oh, how I pray for the sweet lives this book will reach.

Angela Thomas
Bestselling Author, *Choosing Joy*

Pat is an incredible woman with an incredible passion for helping women who hurt. She has surrendered her life to free women from the bondage of their emotional pain. It is our hope that *A Surrendered Life* will give thousands of women renewed hope and a bright future.

Mark Merrill
Author, *All Pro Dad*
President, Family First

Susan Merrill
Director, iMOM

Filmmakers use the craft of storytelling to expose an issue that often needs to be discussed, but afterward people need the right counselors to talk to. So many people who watch *October Baby* desperately need that help, and that is why I'm grateful for Pat Layton. Her work with individuals who have experienced the pain from abortion is unparalleled. And the healing coming out of her ministry for post-abortive people reassures me that those who need to talk are in very good hands.

Andrew Erwin
Filmmaker, *October Baby*

Over 50 million abortions in over 40 years have deeply scarred America and the Christian Church. Pat Layton's courage, candidness and humility in telling her story and the message of Christ's love and healing bring a fresh voice of God's restoration to many who suffer in silence.

David Everitt Sr.
Founder and President, Crisis Pregnancy Centers of Greater Phoenix, Inc.

In my counseling and coaching I have become all too familiar with pain and loss caused by issues from the past. Statistics reveal that for millions of men and women, destructive anxiety, fear, guilt and shame are the result of a past abortion. In *A Surrendered Life*, Pat Layton offers real hope and healing for those who have faced abortion and for those who love them. Drawing from her personal experience, Pat provides eight proven steps that enable those who struggle to move from the loss and pain to healing and freedom.

Georgia Shaffer
Author, *Avoiding the 12 Relationship Mistakes Women Make*
Speaker, PA Licensed Psychologist and Certified Life Coach

A Surrendered Life will lead you on a journey of freedom and hope. Although the topic of abortion can be politically charged, divisive and often avoided in the Church, for the millions of women and men who have experienced one, it is a walk of shame that needs to be redeemed by God's grace. In her book *A Surrendered Life,* Pay Layton shares her story, a transparent eight-step process that leads those who have endured the heartbreak of abortion to a place of redemption and hope. Whether you are part of the estimated 43 percent of women who are hiding the secret of a past abortion or not, chances are high that abortion has touched the life of someone you love. Buy a copy today and discover practical steps and biblical truths that will usher thousands into a place of healing.

Renee Swope
Bestselling Author, *A Confident Heart*
Speaker and Radio Co-host, Proverbs 31 Ministries

I have loved Pat Layton's heart from the first day I met her many years ago. I am praying God will use *A Surrendered Life* to reach every woman who is in pain from a past decision. I believe in this message and the contagious passion that keeps Pat awake at night to help those who are hurting.

Faith Whatley
Director of Adult Ministry, LifeWay Christian Resources

Always be ready to give a . . .

THOUGHTFULRESPONSE
CULTURERELEVANT**BIBLICAL**TRUTH

A SURRENDERED LIFE

 A Thoughtful Approach to
Finding Freedom, Healing and
Hope After Abortion

Patricia K. Layton

BakerBooks
a division of Baker Publishing Group
www.BakerBooks.com

Published by Baker Books
A division of Baker Publishing Group
P.O. Box 6287, Grand Rapids, MI 49516-6287
www.bakerbooks.com

Printed in the United States of America

Library of Congress Cataloging-in-Publication Data is on file at the Library of Congress,
Washington, DC.

Published in association with the literary agency of Legacy LLC, Winter Park, FL, 32789

14 15 16 17 18 19 20 | 10 9 8 7 6 5 4 3 2 1

*This book is dedicated to my Jesus, the One who set me free,
and to the "surrendered life" of our unborn daughter.
Because of His grace, I will hold you.*

*Oh my goodness, Lord. Your majesty overwhelms me.
Your mercy literally allows my life to go on. Your grace covers my utter
failure. Your blessings astound me. Your call on my life brings my knees to
the ground. Your glory draws my arms to the sky. Your anointing makes
me dance. Your vision takes me to repentance. Your death gives me life,
and Your life gives me purpose. Most of all, my Lord, Your love gives me all
that I need. Your Word gives me direction. Your blessing gives me freedom.
Your reflection challenges my pursuit of holiness.
Your supernatural power gives me rest.
I surrender my life to You.*

Pat

Contents

The journey to freedom begins with surrender. We have to make a choice to take hold of all God has for us—sometimes that requires going back to get ahead. Abortion is a physical, emotional and spiritual experience. By making a conscious decision to allow God to walk us through each life connection, we are finally able to obtain complete healing and freedom.

It helps to share your story with others. The enemy uses our failures and secrets to keep us trapped in shame and to weaken our most powerful tool—our testimony.

Abortion is rooted in and thrives upon lies. Lies from the media; lies from political leaders; lies from doctors; lies from counselors and even lies from people we love and trust. The purpose of this chapter is to break the stronghold of the lies that likely propelled our choice for abortion and replace them with the freedom found in truth.

The truth often leads to anger. Understand the healthy spiritual experience of righteous anger. God has given us the emotion of anger to be applied to those actions and events that deny Jesus as Lord and set us up for personal bondage. Learn to replace unhealthy anger with anger that leads to freedom.

By embracing Scripture and biblical paths to forgiveness, you will find that we battle people or laws, but that we have an enemy and his plan is death and destruction. Abortion is a plan of Satan. Forgiveness replaces what Satan means for evil with what God does for good.

Acknowledgments

The beginning of every book holds these very important pages. No book is the work of a single writer. This one is no different, and it may be one of those books that took more than a normal amount of behind-the-scenes support. Without question my thanks begin with Faith Whatley and the amazing team at Lifeway Christian Resources. Without you, I would have never started this journey; and without you, I would not have stuck with it.

Thank you to my precious, patient and very first editor, Dale McCleskey. You are a true renaissance man and a genius. Thank you to my literary agent, D. J. Snell. Sir, you *rock!* Honey hugs to my husband, Mike, and to our family. You are the wind beneath my wings and a daily gift from God. Thank you to Kim Bangs; your faith in my writing and what I have to share makes me want to be better than I am.

Thank you to the national leadership team of Surrendering the Secret. At this moment, we are over 2,000 leaders strong around the world. You ladies (and a few good men!) capture the faith of Esther, the commitment and patience of Ruth for Naomi, the warrior woman in Deborah, and the surrender of Mary. I could go on and on, but mostly, *you* are the hands and feet of Jesus as you minister His love and compassion to those who have endured the heartbreak of abortion.

Introduction

This book is for everyone!
If you have not had an abortion,
a woman in your world has.

An estimated 43 percent of women of childbearing age have had at least one abortion. These women are not necessarily unknown to you. They may be your sisters, your daughters, your friends and even your mothers.

By reading this book, you will benefit in the following ways:

- You will understand why women and men make a choice for abortion;
- You will learn how post-abortion heartbreak may be showing up in your life or the lives of your loved ones;
- You will understand the eight steps to healing from a past abortion;
- You will get equipped with the tools to guide a discussion about the heartbreak of abortion;
- You will learn ways to make a difference in your home, church or community related to this heartbreaking holocaust of life.

Regardless of your personal experience with abortion, the eight-step method of healing and restoration used in *A Surrendered Life* will certainly apply at some level in your own life. You may not have had an abortion, but chances are even greater than the 43 percent statistic that you have had some life-changing loss or heartbreak.

Based on that likelihood, the steps used in *A Surrendered Life* will minister to you and take your walk of faith to a new level.

⇨ ⇨ ⇨ # A Surrendered Life

It was a fabulous Florida day. Springtime. My car windows were rolled down and Christian music blared from my radio speakers. I was singing and praising God out of a new heart filled with hope and thanksgiving. I had surrendered my life to Christ only a few months previously, and within six months of my rebirth my husband and two sons had also turned to Christ. As a result, our lives had dramatically changed, and it seemed that God was suddenly pouring out His blessings on our home and family. Finally, things seemed to be taking a turn for the better after a long season of looming dead-ends and the threat of pending divorce.

Little did I know on that spring day that past secrets, long stuffed away, were about to come crashing in and put my family at risk all over again.

My new Christian journey seemed to be affecting every part of my life, even the radio station sounds coming from my car speakers. I had moved from rock to praise music and was very intrigued by the style of chatter between the radio moderators. They prayed. They quoted Bible verses. They teased about bad habits.

I parked the car and jumped out for a few minutes to run an errand. When I slid back into the driver's seat and started on down the road, the praise music had changed to a talk show. I was shocked to hear a moderator talking with three women who were sharing their stories about past abortions.

I could barely breathe as I listened. My heart raced. *What in the world is this? Abortion! Why are they talking about abortion on a Christian radio station?*

What does God have to do with abortion?

What does abortion have to do with God?

What had happened to my praise music?

Little did I know as I pulled my car to the side of the road to listen that it would change my life forever.

A few months later, after I had successfully stuffed my emotions down again, I strolled into a Christian bookstore with one thing in mind: to find a book that would help me fix my husband! He really needed fixing. We had been Christians for at least a year, and I just knew God still wanted to do a lot of work on him! I ran smack into a display of books all focused on one topic—you guessed it, abortion. I had managed to avoid this topic for more than seven years.

The book standing front and center in the bookstore display was titled *Will I Cry Tomorrow? Healing Post Abortion Trauma*. Oh, my gosh! Here it was again. That word "abortion." In a Christian bookstore! How could that be? I had no idea why I did it, but I grabbed the book, dashed to the register, paid the bill and raced for the door.

Over the next five or six hours, I devoured that book from cover to cover. Although I can remember it as if it were yesterday, it is close to impossible for me to describe the feelings stirring in my heart and mind as I read. Shock, disbelief, fear, disgust and certainly nausea are just a few that come to mind. After finishing the book, I fumbled my way to the bathtub and filled it halfway with very hot water. The rest of the tub I filled with my own hot tears as I sobbed for hours. I wept for my aborted child. I wept for my loss. I wept for the lies. I wept for the author of the book I'd just read. I wept for the abortionists involved in our lives. I wept for the world. I wept for the pain of my Savior, my Lord and Redeemer, Jesus Christ.

When I had finally cried all that I could cry, I handed my heart to God.

Perhaps you can identify with what you've just read. You are familiar with that process in which you allow God to shine His light into the darkest places of your past. As Psalm 139:12 describes, I allowed Him to shine His light on me to make even my darkness light to Him.

Maybe abortion is not your secret, and it's not in your personal past. Maybe there is abuse or abandonment in your past. Childhood brokenness in your family. Rape. Substance abuse. Immorality, adultery, divorce. Or perhaps you are someone who loves someone who has had an abortion. Maybe you are the grandparent of an aborted child, or the brother, sister, friend or neighbor.

In my Women's Conference, "Imagine Me . . . Set Free" (www.
patlayton.net), I have discovered that the process used for post-
abortion recovery is the process God uses, without fail, to set us
free from any past heartbreak or loss. So if you have *not* personally
experienced an abortion, get ready to have God do a work in your
own life as you increase your knowledge for someone else.

It's impossible for you not to know someone who has experienced the horror and heartbreak of a past abortion. After over
40 years of legalized abortion in America, estimates are that one
in three women have had an abortion. More than 50 million lives
have been destroyed. For every single abortion, there is a mother, a
father; grandmothers and grandfathers; brothers, sisters and friends
who are affected.

Wherever you fall in that description, I pray that you will walk
with me on a journey of understanding the truth about abortion
and how its roots can be found in the Bible way back to the book
of Genesis. Most of all, walk with me on a journey through healing
and restoration—a journey toward hope and life.

It matters that you make the journey. It matters to those who
need to hear the truth. It matters to those who didn't hear it in time
and to those whose lives will be rescued because they will.

Let's get started by looking back.

Why You Can't Keep the Past in the Past

Strolling down memory lane can be wonderful. Memories come
and go when we least expect them. The smell of warm baked bread
can take you back to Grandma's house, and you're eight years old
again. Attending a hometown high school reunion inspires you to
drive up and down streets to point out to a spouse or friend your
elementary school, a dear friend's home, or your favorite burger
hangout when you were a kid.

Bad memories—in the same way, and despite our efforts to
suppress them—ebb and flow in our minds and hearts, bringing
pain instead of happiness. Among all the memories we could name,
abortion stands alone.

My most haunting memory concerns an abortion I had when I
was 23 years old. I can remember the smell of the room, the looks
on the faces of the women sitting around the dark reception room,
the sounds of soft lonely tears and the coldness of the building.

Oddly enough, I still remember the dirty tennis shoes worn by the "nurse" who coldly shoved a clipboard intake questionnaire in my direction, and my petrified flight out the door in search of a "nicer abortion." Unlike the sweet memories of elementary school, those darker memories have been seared deeply into my heart and soul for many years.

Traumatic memories have more than a passing impact on our lives. Research confirms my own experience. Not only do abortion memories continue to haunt, but they also substantively damage women and men for years and decades to come.

The thought of going back to deal with emotions I had worked so hard to bury frightened me and seemed overwhelming. What good could come from it? Why would anyone go back? After I spent years trying to put the past behind me, I learned that to experience healing, I had to go back and face my past. Only then did I become free to move into the future.

The Bible contains a story about a woman named Hagar. Although her story does not involve abortion, it does contain many of the emotions engendered by it. Hagar was a woman much like me, and maybe like you. The first parallel of her story with abortion occurs when her dream for family and motherhood did not go the way she planned—the way she had dreamed since she was a little girl.

A woman named Sarai owned Hagar, who was an Egyptian slave. Sarai could not have a child, so she persuaded her husband, Abram, to father a child through the slave girl. After Hagar became pregnant, she began to feel and act superior to her owner:

> Then Sarai said to Abram, "You are responsible for my suffering! I put my slave in your arms, and ever since she saw that she was pregnant, she has looked down on me. May the LORD judge between me and you." Abram replied to Sarai, "Here, your slave is in your hands; do whatever you want with her." Then Sarai mistreated her so much that she ran away from her (Genesis 16:5-6).

We see the second parallel to abortion in Hagar's story when she responded to what she viewed as a hopeless situation by running away as hard and as fast as she could. I don't think she stopped to consider where she might end up or what consequences her choice would bring. She simply responded to her pain and loss with desperation and panic. I can identify with her, because I too have been like Hagar.

Perhaps you, like thousands of women every day, have responded to panic over a pregnancy with the choice to have an abortion. It may have been a choice that seemed to be your only hope, your only option, but desperation doesn't make for sound choices. Just like Hagar, many of us have felt lost, alone and betrayed. So we ran, and with little direction made a choice that would change us forever.

A woman chooses abortion for many reasons: as a response to shame about her behavior and lifestyle patterns, as an act of rebellion or control, or because a husband, boyfriend or parents have given her an ultimatum. Women choose abortion to protect someone else or as an act of confused freedom. Many women have been told that abortion is a simple solution to the problem of an unwanted or unexpected pregnancy. It is the easy out, the quick fix.

Eventually, a woman finds out the truth. Abortion leads to the same place Hagar's choice led her: to run to the middle of nowhere.

My Story

My story wasn't so different. I chose abortion just after my twenty-third birthday. I had lived a life of bad choices and immorality since I was 15. I grew up in an average home with a mother and father who were married as 20-somethings in rural Savannah, Georgia. My parents stayed married for more than 50 years until my dad died—that was nearly 10 years ago. They were blue-collar, God-fearing folk. I have three younger sisters and lots of memories, both good and bad.

My parents also came from fairly average American families neatly woven on the outside but fairly messed up underneath. Their family backgrounds included alcoholism, tobacco and drug addiction, pornography, divorce, adultery and teen pregnancy. This legacy affected their childhoods and mine.

I've learned that family "junk" goes back to Adam and Eve and is truly God's specialty. He uses our personal junk to bring us to good and healed places. My teenage immorality led to a teenage marriage, teenage motherhood, eventual abandonment and, finally, to becoming a single teenage mother of one precious son.

With the help of my parents, I cared for my son and also returned to school and college. I met the next "man of my dreams." The two of us continued in the lifestyle we had both grown accustomed to in the '70s and soon found ourselves with an unplanned pregnancy. The good news was that we were in love and engaged to be married when we found ourselves pregnant. The bad news was that even though I was "in love" and had agreed to be married, I was not "in trust." I had already been left all alone holding a swaddled babe wrapped in a blanket. I was not about to go that route again.

While in college, I had fought diligently for "a woman's right to choose" abortion. During those days, I could wax eloquent about why women should have a right to determine when and if they wanted to have a child. I proclaimed that we ultimately should control "our own bodies." I was so convincing that my opinions had even been published as a pro-choice advocate in a local women's newspaper.

When I discovered I was pregnant, just prior to my wedding day, I made what I thought was a logical and healthy decision to abort. As far as I was concerned, my future husband had no vote. He silently obliged—a choice we would both live to regret.

I told you earlier about my first visit to a newly opened neighborhood abortion clinic that I deemed dirty and dark. That abortion facility left such a nasty taste in my mouth that I decided to approach my own OB/GYN, the one who had delivered my firstborn son, to obtain the "safe and legal" abortion I had fought so hard to legalize.

Just like my future husband, my OB/GYN never questioned my decision. He simply set the date for two weeks after my wedding day. A marriage certificate meant little to me in terms of a man staying for the long haul, so I accepted the date. My husband and I went on our honeymoon pregnant, with a date for an abortion on our calendars soon after we returned. It was not the honeymoon of every little girl's dreams. Neither was the marriage, not for a very long time.

We had planned to drop our son off at kindergarten and arrive at the hospital at 7:00 A.M. (My husband had begun the steps to adopt my son before we married.) I paid the extra money to be put to sleep during the abortion procedure. Even with that, we were told the "procedure" would only take "a few minutes." We planned to pick up our son at school, go get some lunch and move on with life.

The abortion would be our secret.

Instead, I woke up unable to move my body or speak. I had a tube stuck down my throat and a machine breathing for me. While my husband and my parents stood at the foot of my hospital bed, the doctor explained that I'd had an allergic reaction to the anesthesia used to put me to sleep during the procedure. My breathing had stopped during surgery. I had to be admitted to the hospital. My new husband was forced to call my parents to pick up my son from school.

I can still remember the look on the faces of my mom and dad as they stood at the foot of my hospital bed. Shock. Shame. Fear. Loss. My secret was a secret no longer.

My feelings of embarrassment, shame, and even anger followed me out of that hospital. They did not leave me for seven long years.

My parents never said the word "abortion." I never said the word. My husband never said the word. What happened next would close the casket of my heart and affect my life forever.

If you've experienced abortion, you know that the phrase "casket of your heart" is more than a mental picture. Depending on how long ago you had an abortion, or multiple abortions, you have probably kept your secret buried deep inside your heart. Even if someone knows, you probably have never talked about it out loud. You have never wrestled verbally with the who, the what, the when, the where or the why of your choice to abort.

In this book, I want to allow you the opportunity, or maybe I should say, the challenge, of digging into your abortion memory for the purpose of discovering some new things about God. Hagar learned in her situation. She trusted God and braved a return to her past. In the process, Hagar discovered a new identity for God and established her relationship with Him.

I didn't know that choosing to abort my baby wouldn't solve my problem. Rather, abortion created a whole new set of difficulties. Once you begin down the road of abortion, you have to run to the middle of nowhere again and again. Like a modern-day Hagar, you run into the wilderness of fear, shame, abandonment, anger and self-destruction. In a desolate and lonely land, you become numb—a captive to your secret.

Hagar's flight to the desert left her at a spring beside the road. The angel of the Lord met her there and told her to return to Sarai and submit to her authority:

> And the angel also said, "You are now pregnant and will give birth to a son. You are to name him Ishmael (which means 'God hears'), for the LORD has heard your cry of distress..."

Thereafter, Hagar used another name to refer to the LORD, who had spoken to her. She said, "You are the God who sees me."... So Hagar gave Abram a son, and Abram named him Ishmael (Genesis 16:11,13,15, *NLT*).

A Word to Male Readers

If you are a man reading this book, let me salute you. If you are a partner in an abortion, your participation may have ranged from actively pressuring her to abort to being helplessly opposed and excluded. Or you may be in a relationship with a woman who struggles with the results of a past abortion. Please don't feel picked on when I mention the male involvement. I will be talking more specifically about your role and your heart in an abortion decision in "From a Father's Heart: Men and Abortion." But for now, I want you to think on the story of Hagar from a man's perspective.

In the story of Hagar, we see something in Abram that is typical of many men who become involved in abortion. Abram's main mark in the story was extreme passivity. When Sarai hatched the initial scheme, he simply went along. When Sarai regretted the situation, his response was, "Here, your slave is in your hands; do whatever you want with her" (Genesis 16:6).

In dealing with post-abortion recovery, you may face difficult days. Your wife may go through great pain, and she may react negatively toward you. You may be called upon for superhuman patience and love. What you absolutely must not do is become passive, as Abraham did. Actively love her; don't passively withdraw. The kind of relationship you desire will be your reward.

A few other ways abortion affects men:

- Abortion steals and destroys the life and the lineage of a man's legacy and name.

- Abortion violates the core need of a man to provide for and protect his wife and children.

- Abortion separates the heart of a man from the heart of Father God by destroying trust, violating values and building barriers.

Lessons from the Wilderness

As we compare the experience of Hagar's desert to the wilderness we wander today, abortion does not lead to a literal desert. It creates a wilderness we carry in our hearts and minds. When we carry a heavy burden, we naturally feel trapped by the shadows that surround us. Like Hagar, we grow weary and feel ready to give up in despair and shame. As if that weren't enough, both Hagar's story and ours has a villain who always follows us into the wilderness. Instead of seeing the "God who sees me" and the only One who never lets us go, we hear the inner voices of condemnation and shame, and the lying voice of the tempter, Satan.

The amazing news is that God longs to come and rescue us. When God found Hagar, feeling abandoned and hopeless, in the wilderness, He showed her that she must confront her pain and stop trying to mask it. For every woman the mask looks a little different. God wants us to remove our masks—the pain we hide behind—and be set *free*. He sets us free to love, to heal, to forgive and to live.

Some women feel the sting every day of their choice for abortion. Others have completely disconnected from it. No matter how silent your pain, God hears the cry of your heart. He sees you in your desert and feels your pain. God longs for you to look back on that difficult time in your life and, as Hagar did, ask, "Have I truly seen the One who sees me?"

If you are a fellow traveler on the journey of recovery from abortion, I hope you will allow God to use this book in your life. In the next few pages, I will seek to be your guide, your angel in the desert, safely walking back with you to face the secrets, shadows and shame that have kept you from the life God intends for you to live. Just like Hagar, you have a promise that God will personally meet you in your place of need.

You Can Trust the God Who Sees You

If going back to find peace is so crucial for healing, why do we resist? We continue to hesitate for many reasons. We doubt God's heart toward us. After all the pain and struggles, we ask ourselves, *If God is good, how could He have let this happen to me?* Given the way most of us were raised, we also focus on God's judgment with little understanding of His incredible desire and passion for us.

God longs to love you, and you can be assured that your love is safe with Him. His love is like nothing you have ever experienced before. His love is unconditional and eternal. You can rest in God's arms, take comfort in His unfailing love and hold His hand on your journey toward freedom.

You are not alone. Right now, make the choice for freedom. Summon the courage to choose the path of healing and peace. Don't allow your life and dreams to die because of a past mistake.

Think of reading this book and interacting with the journal questions at the end of each chapter as a challenging mountain trek. Now is the time to confront your fear and pain and begin the slow, steady journey to the summit. It takes faith and courage to tackle this mountain, but the view from the top is worth the effort and surrender.

This book will help you get to the summit where the stigma of abortion is gone. In the process, you will find personal healing, or healing for someone you love. I'm going with you. Together you and I can enjoy reconciliation with God and with our unborn children. We can be completely redeemed from a life of secrets, shame and shadows.

In chapter 2, we'll take the first step by looking honestly at post-abortion trauma and how it may be affecting your life. We'll dig into some facts about the physical, social, emotional and spiritual aspects of abortion.

Every man and woman who has chosen abortion as an escape has bought a lie. Lies create secrecy, bondage, darkness and shame. God wants to set you free from all that, but you will have to pursue your freedom through a sometimes uncomfortable journey. You will not be alone. You have an entire team behind the pages of this book. Take a look at the Surrendering the Secret website at www.surrenderingthesecret.com or join us on Facebook and let us know that you have begun this journey.

In Luke 1:79 (*AMP*), we read that the plan of God is "to shine upon and give light to those who sit in darkness and in the shadow of death, to direct and guide our feet in a straight line into the way of peace." God wants to direct your feet into that light and peace—His complete peace. It is a peace that doesn't allow anything to shame you or make you feel like you have felt as a result of past heartbreaks. He wants you to be free from all insecurity and fear.

Through the pages of this book, you and I are going to take a peace journey together by a process that has been setting people free for more than 20 years. We are about to step out together to stand up and shout out to the world, "*I am free,* I am healed, and I am whole! My God has seen my pain and my shame and He has rescued me. Jesus is my refuge. He is my place of shelter and my only hope. I can trust Him to protect me." Isaiah 41:13 (*AMP*) records these words: "For I the Lord your God hold your right hand; I am the Lord, Who says to you, Fear not; I will help you!"

Heart to Heart from Pat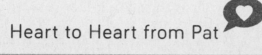

You have my book in your hands! When I let that truth grab my head and heart, it blows me away. *A book like this changed my entire life forever.* A book like this saved my marriage. God used a book like this to call me into full-time ministry.

I clearly remember the day I picked up that book about abortion. It was in the summer of 1985. I had just recently given my life to Christ. As I shared earlier, within a few months, God also drew my husband and my two sons to Himself.

I was immediately passionate about God's Word, and I strived to learn all I could about living my life for Him. I was also on a bit of a quest to get my husband in "biblical order" when I journeyed out that day to the local Christian bookstore. I planned to look for some books to help him learn how to be a better husband. Much to my surprise, standing right smack in the entryway of that bookstore was a display for the book *Will I Cry Tomorrow? Healing Post Abortion Trauma* by Dr. Susan Stanford. The book was Dr. Stanford's story—her abortion experience as a young college student. I was brand-new in my Christian walk, but I knew immediately in my heart that God had placed that book in my path. A quest to fix my husband was about to rock my world.

That was more than 20 years ago. Little did I know how that book would change my life! I truly believe that this book is going to change your life as well. You are about to experience an encounter with God, like I did.

Scripture says that the plan of God is "to shine upon and give light to those who sit in darkness and in the shadow of death, to direct and guide our feet in a straight line into the way of peace" (Luke 1:79, *AMP*). I have found this to be completely true. I have recorded times when God has wonderfully directed my feet and brought me into the way of peace.

Let me tell you about my personal prayer journal, which I have used for 30-plus years. A few years ago, I started to take the time to cover each journal with magazine pictures, Scripture and claims of faith for the things going on in my life. When I start a new journal, I always write the beginning date on the cover and the date I close the last page.

Here are a few thoughts from my journal written the morning that I arrived in the breathtaking Appalachian Mountains to film the *Surrendering the Secret* Bible study videos in the hot summer of 2007.

> Oh Lord, You have placed me in many amazing spots to write in my journal. I have written in it through many rough growing stages, many life journeys, many praise reports. Salvation is in my journals, new births, deaths, broken friendships and new friendships. My life, rather, my daily morning places are in these pages. But, *wow*, Lord, these next few days will record a life passage that I believe, aside from my marriage and my children being given life, is one of the reasons I was born. Your Word says that you created, knit and fashioned me in my mother's womb; that You, in fact, knew the days of my life. Jeremiah tells me that You actually have a plan for me. You knew that I would choose the wild life of youth, Lord. You knew there was not enough of You in me to direct my paths Your way. But even then, You never stopped watching me; I never got away from Your grip. In some ways, the thought is chilling to my bones. The things that You saw me do, Lord, the choices that You saw me make. All the while, instead of turning away in disgust and anger, You—Holy Bridegroom—continued to woo me, to pursue me, to call me. I remember that the day I stopped running, we were not in a pretty place, were we, Lord? It was not a pretty scene. But even there, in the depth of my sin, You called into my heart, "Come away, daughter, follow Me out of your darkness. Follow My voice and I will lead you to great and mighty places and experiences. To beautiful, majestic views with cool breezes and quiet peace beyond your dreams!" You did it, Lord! You filled my entire life with great and mighty places and experiences and have blessed me beyond my dreams.

In what place are you right now? God wants to direct your feet into that same light and peace, into complete peace, so that nothing shames you, nothing makes you feel like you have felt as a result of past heartbreaks. He wants you to be free from all insecurity and fear.

I cannot express in mere words all that my heart feels as I greet you. I have prayed for you for so long that I truly feel like I would know you in the grocery store or on the street corner, just by the connection of our hearts. I wish that I could be where you are right now so that I could physically wrap my arms around you and calm your fears.

I remember the day that I publicly stepped out as you have stepped out. I could hold in my secret no longer. That day I knew that somehow my abortion secret was keeping my walk with God from moving forward; it was keeping me in a place of shame and emptiness that I deeply feared no other person on earth could understand. After all, I had no other choice; I had to do it. I fully believed that I'd had an abortion for the protection and benefit of everyone around me. But somehow, deep in my most hidden emotions, something was very wrong. Something important was missing. My one and only purpose is to encourage you, to love you, to cheer you on. I want to promise you that I am going to walk every step of this journey with you. You are not alone.

God wants us whole. He wants us healed—every bit of us, even our secrets. Especially our secrets.

In the next seven chapters, we are going to make believe that we are climbing a mountain with the goal of experiencing a glorious view from the top. Now, I have to admit that I am not the most athletic person you will ever meet. (I think the best place for hiking boots is in the mall.) So, if I can do this, you can do this too. We just have to remember God's words of promise: "I am the Lord who says to you, fear not, I will help you."

This may be the bravest moment in your entire life. I am so proud of you, and I want to promise you that if you stick this out and finish this journey, you will get to that virtual mountain peak as a new woman who fully understands the mighty love God has for you. He is pursuing you. You are His little girl; you are His daughter, His treasured possession. He knows where you have been and He knows where He wants to take you!

I will see you again!

A Note about *Surrendering the Secret* tools, *Imagine Me. . . Set Free* and other ministry resources available to you!

Surrendering the Secret

A Surrendered Life is supported by a Bible study book and accompanying videos called *Surrendering the Secret* published by Lifeway. The chapters and video content in those products run parallel with this book and can be used together or independently.

Surrendering the Secret is a powerful tool for group or one-on-one Bible study. It has many interactive sessions that will help you process some of what you are reading in *A Surrendered Life* and offers some experiential exercises that will support your healing journey. I hope you will grab yourself a brand-new spiral notebook as your hiking companion on this spiritual journey.

At the end of each chapter, I'll be leaving you with some questions to help you process what you have read and apply it to your own story. Take some time to allow these questions to stir your memories and your heart enough to begin this journey. I know this effort will require a lot of trust. I ask you to trust me as another woman who has been where you have been and where you are going. More important, it will require trusting God to hold you tight and show you His purpose for leading you to this study.

In addition to the Bible study, we offer a variety of personal healing retreats and online ministry tools. We maintain a website and a resource list of leaders all over the world who have been trained to facilitate *Surrendering the Secret* Bible studies and healing groups. Go to www.patlayton.net to find a *Surrendering the Secret* Bible study event or to find a leader in your community.

Imagine Me. . . Set Free

Once you have stepped into the healing and restoration found through *Surrendering the Secret,* God often calls you into a deeper encounter with Him as He uncovers the next step of your journey and draws you more deeply into His plan for your future.

Living Free: Imagine Me. . . Redeemed, Restored, Renewed. . . Set Free is a ministry program offered throughout the year in a variety of formats:

- *Church hosted "Freedom Weekends"* are held around the nation, throughout the year, for anywhere from 100 to 500 women. The event is an interactive adventure that begins on a Friday night and continues all day Saturday. Women join together to take a journey through Psalm 139, using a customized tool called a "Freedom Flower" that helps women embrace healing and renewal. We call it "Peace with the Past, Purpose in the Present and Passion for the Future."
- *Freedom Quest* is an intimate encounter with God that is held at a beautiful retreat setting. The en counter is set up for a small group of fewer than 25 women. These retreats are held three to four times each year and are by application only. The event is personalized for your particular needs and is a walk through the Freedom Flower used in the *Imagine Me. . .* Freedom Weekends.
- *One-on-One Freedom Flower Coaching* provided by Pat and a group of trained facilitators.

Information on all of these *Living Free* options can be found at www.patlayton.net. Also watch for Pat's new book *Life Unstuck.*

JOURNAL TIME

You may or may not be reading this book as someone who has experienced a past abortion.

The journal suggestions at the end of each chapter will generally reference an abortion decision. But if you have not had an abortion, use this time of reflection to respond to God as He has prompted your heart by what you have read and learned. Substitute your personal story in place of the abortion questions; or if you are reading this book to help someone you love, try to complete the answers as best you can.

1. Have you ever experienced a Hagar moment? Has there been a time in your life when running away seemed to be your only option? Record your experience and God's response. (You may want to use a journal to write your answers.)

   _____

   _____

   _____

2. Find a quiet and safe place to pray and ask God to take your hand and walk back in time with you. Here we go:
   • Where did your abortion/s take place? Write your story.

   _____

   _____

   _____

   • Who was with you?

   _____

   _____

   _____

   • Who knew what was going on for you?

   _____

   _____

   _____

- How did you handle the procedure?

- The aftercare?

- How did you deal with your emotions after the procedure was over?

Close your first journal entry with a short prayer asking God to lead you. Ask Him to hold you and direct you into what He wants you to learn from this, and ask Him to begin to show you how you will use your testimony to make Him known in the world.

2

Sharing the Secret: Going Backward to Move Forward

A woman has what may be the greatest power a human can possess—the power to choose to grow and protect a life created in her womb by God or take action that will terminate that life. The mind can barely comprehend the reality that two tiny cells can come together in a moment of passion, lust or ignorance and create a living human being. That new person, if nothing is done to stop his or her development, will draw breath from the minute he or she is born and will change the world simply by being. The same is true for the loss of a life. Whether or not anyone notices, the loss of a life changes the entire world. The Bible teaches that God created every human being, whether male or female, with a purpose, a destiny, an assignment.

Next to the impact on the child, the mother suffers the most profound damage from abortion. When a woman chooses abortion, a piece of her very self, and a piece of her heart, dies. That loss cannot be ignored, at least not forever. No matter how hard she tries to deny the event, at some point, for some reason, the memory returns.

In this chapter, we will focus on breaking the power of silence and secrecy. The past has held us captive for too long as a result of a chosen abortion. Let me tell you a story to illustrate how the silence begins.

I was about eight years old the first time I remember getting caught in a lie. My family was at a cookout on the beach when suddenly my sister started crying. (Insert a mental image of my most innocent look here.) I had *no idea* what had happened. At least that was the report I gave my mother.

Little did I know that my mother had watched me drop a Fiddler Crab into my sister's swimsuit. The crab had mostly scared my sister, but she acted as if I was an ax murderer. I got into some major deep water with my mom for lying. Paradoxically, I was the one who was permanently scarred. Lies hurt others, but like slow-dripping acid, they eat us alive from the inside out.

No one has to teach a child to lie. In our fallen world, deception is the norm rather than the exception. We've practiced deception since Eve in the garden. People give many excuses. Some people lie for their own selfish gain; but I think most of the time we lie out of fear to avoid exposure, loneliness or vulnerability.

Children learn quickly that lying can get them into trouble. As a result, they either choose to be more truthful or they resort to more lies, sneaking around, or clamming up in silence. As adults, we continue these same patterns. We all have secrets—things we've done that we hope no one will ever know about. In the words of the apostle Paul, "For everyone has sinned; we all fall short of God's glorious standard" (Romans 3:23, *NLT*).

Why Our Enemy Revels in Secrets and Silence

Every one of us hides something we don't want others to know about—something we're ashamed for them to know. The villain in everyone's life story, Satan, knows that as long as he can keep us bound by our silence and secrets, he can keep us from the freedom God offers. As long as Satan can keep us isolated and separated from others, we automatically remain in bondage. A slogan in recovery programs says it well: *We're as sick as our secrets.*

As we learn to live in silence and secrecy, many of us end up with a stockpile of hurts we've buried deep down inside. The only way to overcome and to live free of those hurts is to learn to recognize the lies we've accepted as truth. As we root out each lie, we begin to replace it with the truth. When Jesus said the truth would set us free (see John 8:32), He expressed a double meaning. In the ultimate sense, we only find freedom in the person of Christ, who *is* the truth (see John 14:6). In a smaller sense, we find freedom bit by bit as we drain the lies of their power and expose them to the truth.

Satan uses lies about God, our self-worth, other people and the world to keep us limping along with old infected wounds and trapped in unhealthy ways of living. Culture bombards us with myths and deceptions about sex, love and life. That's why Jesus spoke strongly about the deceiver who plants so many lies in our world. Jesus said of the devil, "He was a murderer from the beginning and has not stood in the truth, because there is no truth in him. When he tells a lie, he speaks from his own nature, because he is a liar and the father of liars" (John 8:44).

The apostle Peter knew great failure and shame. After claiming special commitment and loyalty to Jesus, this brash apostle denied Him only hours later. Peter learned the hard way what he later wrote of the devil: "Be serious! Be alert! Your adversary the Devil is prowling around like a roaring lion, looking for anyone he can devour" (1 Peter 5:8).

The devil seeks to isolate and slowly destroy us. He is the master deceiver. With the benefit of millennia spent watching human nature, Satan takes advantage of our tendency to try to escape. He knows that we will usually run away like Hagar did, rather than make the bold choice to confront our pain.

Unwilling to face our intense emotions or take responsibility for our actions, we let our burdens become our identity. We accept lies about ourselves and about God. In the process, we settle for survival in place of real life. Keeping the secret allows the pain to slowly eat away at us. As a result, we often seek to self-medicate to get some relief from the pain. Other times, we experience the opposite. Because we feel nothing, we use self-destructive behaviors just to be able to feel something.

What about you? What means have you used to escape the pain or to feel something through the numbness? Common options include literally medicating with drugs (the most common of which is alcohol), behaviorally medicating through self-destructive behaviors and, in our darkest moments, attempting suicide.

When tempted by these ploys and behaviors, you *must* remember the reality of who your enemy is. Satan strategically uses the wounds in your life. He strives to distort your identity. He knows your vulnerabilities and takes advantage of your weaknesses. If Satan can keep you feeling worthless, feeling guilty or keep your mind and heart under his influence, he can keep you from the glory God intended.

The Enemy's Strategy to Keep You Down

Satan seeks to separate you from the intimacy God wants you to have with Him. That's why the Deceiver continually whispers lies about who you are and who God is; lies about God's heart toward you and the intimacy God wants you to share with Him. Satan employs a three-part strategy to steal, kill and destroy. The strategy looks like this:

- *Step One:* In the normal course of every person's life, things happen that hurt, shame, or cause us to be afraid. The more severe these events, the greater their impact can be. A high-stress pregnancy followed by abortion rates high on any scale of such events.
- *Step Two:* The pain you experience causes a wound. If left untreated (no healing or restoration), infection sets in. Infection comes in the form of feelings of rejection; lack of self-worth; or worse, feelings of self-hatred. You respond to such feelings with hopelessness, depression or abuse of substances or people.
- *Step Three:* The enemy of life begins to whisper lies in your ear. If you don't have the voice of truth to offset the lies of the Evil One, you begin to believe the lies. As time goes by, you even begin to speak the lies to yourself as truth: *No one loves me. I am a nobody. I am alone. I deserve this treatment. It was my fault.* Most of all, you begin to believe that people will never accept you, and God will never forgive you.

All too often, Satan succeeds in building within you a distorted view of God and the world. At that point, the enemy has won. He then has control of your thoughts. Your thoughts in turn control your actions. You have fallen into his trap.

No wonder Scripture instructs, "Above all else, guard your heart, for everything you do flows from it" (Proverbs 4:23, *NIV*). Jesus clearly described how powerful are the core beliefs of our hearts in directing our lives and our legacies: "It is what comes from inside that defiles you. For from within, out of a person's heart, come evil thoughts" (Mark 7:20-21, *NLT*).

Break the Silence and Break Free

The battle of life happens mostly in our minds. We have an enemy who fights dirty, and our secrets give him ammunition. He continually proves himself more than happy to use our secrets against us. One of the most practical things any of us can do to thwart his plan is to break the silence. When we open our secrets to the light of shared truth, we literally take the stick out of the devil's hands—the one he has been using to beat us black and blue.

So how do you break the silence and get free? How do you over-come years and years of enemy strongholds over your thoughts, beliefs and life? The answer will scare you at first: You need to tell your story.

You need to speak out the hurts and pain. You need to expose the darkness to the light. This step has a purpose far beyond re-opening old wounds. Honesty builds community.

God never intended us to struggle alone. People need each other, and we were designed for strong relationships. Amazing things oc-cur when two or more people grasp hands and hearts and share their pain together. God is in their midst. He does amazing things with those who are humble and open to His supernatural surgery of the heart. Through God's power, we find recovery, freedom and healing.

Solomon, the wisest human king ever, described our need for each other in the book of Ecclesiastes. He said a person without a companion experiences no end of struggles, but "two are better than one because they have a good reward for their efforts. For if either falls, his companion can lift him up; but pity the one who falls without another to lift him up. Also, if two lie down together, they can keep warm; but how can one person alone keep warm? And if somebody overpowers one person, two can resist him. A cord of three strands is not easily broken" (Ecclesiastes 4:9-12).

We all need someone we can trust and with whom we can share our story. We need someone who will listen and not judge. We need someone who will keep our story confidential and who will pray with and for us. This need isn't limited to those of us with abortion in our past; but the more shameful our past seems to us, the more desperate the need.

Because the very thought of surrendering our secret shame frightens us so, we need to consider what disclosure does and does not mean. I am not suggesting that transparency means telling everyone everything. Healthy boundaries mean that we disclose ourselves appropriately to the right people, in the right way, at the right time. It most definitely does not mean opening ourselves to unsafe people.

A daunting problem for many of us was how to find the safe person or group where we could share our pain. Sometimes we don't even know what a safe person looks like. As someone said, we need someone who will know all about us and love us still. We need others who will love us unconditionally but also tell us the truth.

If you already have that kind of relationship, you're a fortunate person. You're in a very distinct and blessed minority. Most people desperately long for such a deep relationship. If you are like most of us, you will have to seek out that kind of support.

There is great benefit from sharing your experiences through specialized groups outside of your regular friends. A homogenous group of people who have shared similar experiences can hear your story with understanding. In a purely pragmatic sense, openness with strangers can simply be easier. Many churches and local pregnancy centers offer counseling and support for both men and women. You may want to join a *Surrendering the Secret* Bible study. To find out more about the study and possible groups in your area, go to www.patlayton.net.

Those who have an abortion in their past often are absolutely terrified of being found out. They probably chose abortion in the first place to keep a secret. They feared the pregnancy would be discovered. Fear continues to be one reason why many women and men have guarded their secret for years. Guarding the secret means they have fallen for a great deception.

Who do you really protect by holding on to the secret? You are covering up the Deceiver's lie that abortion doesn't hurt you. You are reinforcing society's belief that the choice doesn't hurt women. Remaining silent keeps you in the darkness of the lie; freedom comes from exposing it.

Please understand: God's desire is not to expose you and then leave you feeling alone and vulnerable. Rather, God knows that your confession exposes the darkness to the light. Once your secret is in the light, God can do His healing work. You have a protecting and caring Father who covers His children with grace, not shame. Be courageous; expose the enemy's lie under the protection of God.

I'll Go First

Not long after becoming a believer in Christ, I began to sense that God was calling me to confess my abortion. As a new Christian,

I couldn't imagine why God was bringing me down this path. Why was He asking me to share that of all things? After all, I had just started a new future in Him. I had just asked Christ into my heart at a women's retreat. I had made all new Christian friends and was changing all of the things about my life that I knew should be changed.

I knew I had a way to go. I had a lot to make right. I'd come to the end of myself and given my big, fat mess of a life to Jesus. At that point of surrender, my marriage was in shambles and my kids were being thrown back and forth between my husband and me. My job was filled with dishonesty and immorality. In the middle of these present problems, I couldn't imagine why God would have me concentrate on something that had happened seven years earlier. Weren't we supposed to forget the past and concentrate on the future?

I had never talked to anyone about my abortion. It was secret—something I barely remembered myself. Yet, I had no doubt God was leading me.

I called one of my new Bible study girlfriends and asked her to meet me for lunch. My heart pounded in my chest and my head felt like it was spinning. I saw my friend Ann, with her sparkling smile, bounding toward me from the tearoom parking lot. No getting away this time, it was too late to duck. Ann instinctively reached for my hands as I began to tremble and tears ran down my cheeks. I had never been so scared in my life.

Ann was my new best friend. She first approached me at the church ladies' retreat. She had invested in me, pulling me into her circle of beautiful, godly women, and had coached me in my new walk with God. Ann was the person who taught me how to pray out loud. She was the one who planted within me a hunger for the Bible and a desire for intimacy with God. She continued to walk with me step by step through the metamorphosis of my new life in Jesus.

In the few months that had passed since I surrendered to God at that ladies' retreat, my life had turned around so beautifully. My marriage, my children and even my music had been transformed by the new life Jesus offers. My spirit and emotions had gone from depression to hope-filled. Little did I suspect that this incredible walk into new life with God would lead me to a crossroads where I found myself face-to-face with a dark secret from my old life. Not only had I hidden this secret from the world, but I had also stuffed it so deep inside that I was hiding it from myself.

As I clutched Ann's hands that day in the tearoom, I felt like my newly found peace and joy were about to be demolished; but I knew that God was asking me to surrender my secret, just as He'd asked that I surrender my life to Him.

The secret swelled so fiercely in my heart that I was about to burst. Turmoil and panic gripped my chest because I had no idea what Ann would say or how exposing this dark part of my past would affect our friendship. Ann and all my new friends at church seemed so godly and good. What would they think of me? What would they think about the awful thing I had done?

I know you want to read what happened next, and I promise to share more about it later. You've taken a huge step by reading this far. Let my friend Sheri's words encourage you to take that first important step of telling the secret:

> I remember being in your shoes not so long ago and thinking that this was not going to work. Opening up would be impossible for anyone who hurt like I did over my abortion. It was just too personal. The amazing thing I discovered through the process was that I was not alone in my pain and sorrow.
>
> The decision to heal must come from your heart, no one can force you into anything. Start courageously, and finish strong!
>
> Your sister in Christ,
> Sheri

Heart to Heart from Pat

Wow! This has been another tough chapter challenge, hasn't it? Not only have you confronted a secret that has been hidden deep in your heart, but you have also spent some time looking at how that secret has stolen freedom from you. The Father of Lies, Satan, has used that painful choice to take your own life in so many ways.

During the past 20 years that I have been ministering to women who have been sold the lie of abortion, I have never stopped feeling shocked or heartbroken at the things women are told. At the crisis pregnancy center I founded in Tampa, we receive thousands of contacts each year from women who are facing an unwanted or unplanned pregnancy. They come to us having heard all sorts of false information about the development of their unborn child, the simplicity of the abortion procedure and the ease of their recovery.

You have learned many statistics this past week, some coming directly from the abortion industry itself. You looked at some factual information that women need to know but have no one to tell them. If we are bound up in our abortion secrets, how will other women ever hear the truth about the pain and horror of an abortion procedure? How will they hear the truth about the so-called "quick recovery" that follows abortion? How will they know what God says about abortion if the church remains silent in our wounds?

I was so very ignorant of any of those facts when I chose to have an abortion. All I could think about at the time was my shame and my need for a quick fix that no one would ever have to know about.

At the end of chapter 1, there were questions to ask yourself and to ask God about how you are feeling after all that you have been reading. It is one thing to remember details of your abortion experience, but it is quite another to actually share the details with someone else. I cannot even count all of the women I have ministered post-abortion healing to over a period of many years, but every single time, I think of all of the women and all of the babies who have been damaged and destroyed by this destructive choice.

You have studied a new term called "Post Abortion Trauma" and seen the many ways that choosing an abortion can affect your life even beyond the loss of your unborn child. I am certain that you have identified many things you have experienced firsthand. This is a difficult journey that will lead not only to your freedom but also to the freedom your truth-telling will bring to many other women and young girls who are all at risk for believing the same lies.

In the next chapter, I will share a poem I wrote shortly after reading what God had to say about the unborn child in Psalm 139. I am sure you will relate to some of the feelings I express in my poem. I wrote it in 1986, just two years after I came to know the Lord. God has done so much in my life since those days. He has actually used my pain to minister to others. He has revealed His healing love in my life and has set me on a course that seems to get richer and richer with each new day. As I have studied Psalm 139, it has become one of my favorite passages of Scripture, and I hear it as describing not only my precious lost child, but also myself. And now you know it describes *you*.

I pray this scriptural prayer over you as you continue reading:

Thank You, my Lord, that You have searched my dear sister and You know her. You know when she sits down and when she stands; You understand her thoughts from far away. You, Lord, observe her travels and her rest and are aware of all of her ways. Before a word is on her tongue, Lord, You know it. You have encircled her and placed Your hand upon her. This extraordinary knowledge is beyond our ability to understand. Where can she go to escape Your spirit, Lord? Where can she flee from Your presence? If she goes to heaven, You are there; if she makes her bed in the depths, You are there. If she rises on the wings of the dawn, if she settles on the far side of the sea, even there Your hand will guide her and Your right hand will hold her fast.

If she says surely the darkness will hide me, and the light become night around me, even the darkness will not be dark to You; the night will shine like the day, for darkness is light to You, Lord. For You, most high God, have knit her together in her mother's womb, she is fearfully and wonderfully made; Your works are wonderful. She knows that full well. Her frame was not hidden from You when she was made in the secret places, when she was woven together in the depths of the earth; Your eyes saw her unformed body. All the days ordained for her were written in Your book before even one of them came to be.

How precious are Your thoughts, O God, how vast is the sum of them. Were I to count them, they would outnumber the grains of sand. When she wakes up, Lord, she is still with You. Oh, Lord, if only You would slay the wicked and the bloodthirsty men; they speak of You with evil intent and misuse Your name. She hates those who hate You, O Lord. Search her, O Lord, see if there is any offensive way in her, and lead her in the way everlasting. I thank You, Holy God. Amen!

God is leading you today, sweet friend. As the psalm says, He is watching you and leading you. You can trust Him.

Journal Time

Take some time to think and pray about who knows about your abortion. Is that person (or persons) someone you can trust to share this experience? WARNING: I strongly recommend that you do *not* contact an old boyfriend or ex-spouse during this process unless God gives you clear direction to do that and mature Christian leaders confirm it. Ask God for direction and leading toward a Christian friend, spouse or ministry leader.

If you are not ready for that step, take the time to write your story in your journal. The previous chapter's questions should have gotten you started remembering the story of your abortion experience.

If you have never had an abortion, take this time to understand the difficulty of this step by considering a past "secret" of your own.

Take your time. Ask God to help you, and allow our online community to be a resource and support to you.

Here are some additional questions to stir your thoughts and help you "Share Your Story" either in person or in writing.

1. What were your life circumstances and relationships like at the time of your abortion?

2. Was there anyone in your life whom you felt you could completely trust?

3. When or how did the idea of abortion come to mind? What other options did you consider?

4. Describe your abortion experience.

_____
_____
_____
_____

5. Describe thoughts and feelings that you recall before, during and after the abortion.

_____
_____
_____
_____

6. What about you changed the day of the abortion?

_____
_____
_____

3

What Is the Truth?

Abortion advocates present abortion to women as a quick fix, an easy out, an over-in-a-minute answer for an unplanned, unwanted pregnancy. When a woman enters an abortion clinic, she is in the passion of crisis. Panic, shame or fear often overrules the facts. Women who choose abortion have been compared to an animal willing to chew its own leg off to free itself from the jaws of a trap. I know, because I was one of those women.

Back in 1986, after discovering what God had to say about life and abortion, and during my own walk to healing, I wrote the following poem:

> I knew before they spoke it,
> As women often do,
> That a life had formed inside me
> Though I prayed it not be true.
>
> In an instant, I was not alone,
> Fear stood by constantly,
> It attacked my thoughts in dark, black moods,
> *How could this have happened to me?*
>
> I do not want this baby,
> There is no other way;
> "GET RID OF IT" were words I heard
> The price seemed small to pay.
>
> The whiteness of the ceiling,
> Bright lights and sharp cold air
> Are vivid in my memories,
> I never knew I'd care.

Years went past with only fleeting thoughts
Of what "it" might have been.
It never even dawned on me that
Murder is a sin.

It never seemed to me that way,
Until one awful night,
A nightmare broke into my sleep,
I screamed and cried with fright.

I could see the Lord beside me,
By that table, in that place,
I saw His eyes, and heard His voice,
And tears streamed down His face.

In a broken voice He said to me,
"My daughter, tell me why
I worked with love to make that child
For you to let it die?"

Since that meeting with the Lord,
He's healed my wounds and sins,
But I'll never be completely healed
Until ABORTION ENDS.

In chapter 2, we discussed the process of deception Satan uses to rob us of freedom and an abundant life. The Bible calls Satan the father of lies (see John 8:44). Satan never stops pouring his twisted deception into our world. Our acceptance of his lies gives Satan his best ammunition. When we fall for and then perpetrate deceit bit by bit, we take on the character of the evil one.

God hates lies for at least two reasons: They represent the very opposite of His character, and they hurt those He loves. Scripture clearly states God's opinion of all things false: "Lying lips are detestable to the LORD, but faithful people are His delight" (Proverbs 12:22). Proverbs 6:16-19 tells us, "There are six things the LORD hates, seven that are detestable to Him: haughty eyes, a lying tongue, hands that shed innocent blood, a heart that devises wicked schemes, feet that are quick to rush into evil, a false witness who pours out lies and a person who stirs up conflict in the community" (Proverbs 6:16-19, NIV).

God didn't put those statements in His Word to make us miserable or to control us. He seeks to guide and protect us by setting boundaries for our own good. We learned from John 8:32 that the truth will set us free. No lie ever has or ever will bring freedom. Whether people lie for their own gain, to protect themselves or because they have personally bought into the deception, lies cause serious damage. The power of a lie bears fruit when we act on it as truth.

Lies have eroded truth in many places in our world. We have built a world culture very much like the one described in Jeremiah: "They make ready their tongue like a bow, to shoot lies. . . They go from one sin to another; they do not acknowledge me, declares the LORD. Everyone has to be on guard against his friend. Don't trust any brother, for every brother will certainly deceive, and every friend spread slander. Each one betrays his friend; no one tells the truth" (Jeremiah 9:3-5).

To find freedom, we must build a microcosm of truth away from this world of deception. We begin that process in our relationship with God and with at least one trustworthy fellow human.

If you, like me, face the aftermath of an abortion, consider the circumstances that led to your original decision. What messages did you hear? Did the people closest to you tell you that it was okay and that it was your only choice? Did billboards, Internet or media articles influence you? As part of your healing, you must identify what you believed when you chose abortion so that you can begin to understand some of the effects that may have followed the abortion.

Post-Abortion Emotions and Behavior

Statistics tell us that most abortions occur for women ages 18 to 24. That's the time of her life when a woman is exploring many of her values and moral codes. When I chose abortion, I was in a season of making choices and practicing behaviors that I had never truly chosen but, more accurately, followed. Even when women choose abortion later in life, they indicate that they made the decision outside of, or in spite of, deeply held moral values and beliefs.

For many women, and men, the first emotion after an abortion is immediate relief that they are no longer burdened with the unwanted pregnancy. Research indicates, however, that this short-lived relief is frequently replaced by guilt, shame, secrecy, sadness and regret. The unexpected reactions to an abortion decision are commonly referred to as post-abortion trauma. Approximately 40 percent of post-abortive women experience intense traumatic responses, but statistics reveal that 80 percent will experience some level of symptoms. Some psychologists believe the statistic is actually as high as 100 percent of post-abortive women who suffer some measure of trauma.

Here are some alarming statistics on the negative effects of abortion:[1]

92% of women who have had an abortion experience emotional deadening
63% experience denial
58% battle nightmares
86% experience anger or rage
56% develop suicidal feelings
86% fear others finding out
53% engage in drug abuse
82% experience intense feelings of loneliness or isolation
39% have eating disorders

The Alan Guttmacher Institute, a division of Planned Parenthood, estimates that 43 percent of American women will have an abortion by age 45. The Institute says that half of all pregnancies in the U.S. are unintended; out of those, 4 in 10 pregnancies will end in abortion. In the U.S. alone, more than 1.5 million abortions are performed each year, making abortion one of the most common elective surgical procedures performed on women today.[2]

The same statistical research indicates some of the responses to the question "Why do Women Get Abortions?"[3]

75% said their baby would interfere with their lives
66% said they couldn't afford a child
50% didn't want to be a mother at the time
 4% had a doctor who said their health would worsen with the baby
 1% had a fetal abnormality
 1% were victims of rape or incest

The effects reported by men whose wives or girlfriends had an abortion are not entirely different from the aftershocks suffered by women. In the late Guy Condon's heartfelt book *Fatherhood Aborted*, he lists the following symptoms of male post-abortion trauma:

- You have difficulty with commitment.
- You dodge authority.
- You have no solid sense of authority.
- You work to impress moral leaders.
- You keep women at bay.
- You have trouble bonding.
- You fear impending tragedy.
- You don't own your mistakes.
- You feel inadequate as a leader.

To Make Right Decisions You Need the Truth

Obviously, abortion brings unexpected consequences. Both women and men discover the painful and damaging results only after the fact. If neither media nor medical professionals provide the complete truth, how are Christians to know what abortion truly costs? How does abortion truly impact a society or culture? Understanding the statistics along with the truth and direction found in the Word of God, we can make an informed decision concerning abortion.

Considering the statistics, abortion clearly does not represent the best choice, the only choice or the choice without complications. It runs opposite to the value the Word of God places on a human life.

Life Begins with God

Heated debate rages about when life begins. The very question comes from our world's desire to justify abortion. The idea that life begins at birth or somewhere in the gestation process gives abortion advocates what they believe to be intellectual grounds to justify the procedure. However, the very idea violates both science and Scripture.

The scientific facts about the beginning of life simply show that life does not begin in the birth process at all. Life clearly began long ago. Creationists believe that life began with God's work. Evolutionists believe that life began through random processes. Both positions agree absolutely about a key point: *Life began in the distant past and is passed on from one generation to the next.* Once we recognize that simple fact, no question exists about when life is passed from parent to child.

The Bible doesn't say a great deal about when life begins, probably because the question is so artificial. The writers of Scripture could never have conceived of modern attitudes about a baby as a burden rather than a blessing. When the Bible does speak of prenatal life, the message is clear. The psalmist wrote,

> Oh yes, you shaped me first inside, then out; you formed me in my mother's womb. I thank you, High God—you're breathtaking! Body and soul, I am marvelously made! I worship in adoration—what a creation! You know me inside and out, you know every bone in my body; You know exactly how I was made, bit by bit, how I was sculpted from nothing into something. Like an open book, you watched me grow from conception to birth; all the stages of my life were spread out before you, the days of my life all prepared before I'd even lived one day (Psalm 139:13-16, *THE MESSAGE*).

Earlier, I stated that a large percentage of abortions occur to young women. I was an exception; I gave birth to my first child at 18. Years later, when faced with a choice for abortion with my second pregnancy, the stage of development of my unplanned baby was the least of my concerns. I had never studied nor really considered the development process of my unborn child. I was more worried about what I would do with a born child than spending any time learning the stages of an unborn one.

I have counseled thousands of women over the past 25 years and have rarely encountered one who allowed her thoughts to consider the development of the baby. Few of us have had the opportunity to voice our thoughts and questions. Our society considers such concerns untouchable. We can't understand the amazing elements of creating a person's soul, but even the physical development of the baby is beyond what most of us would imagine.

1. At 21 days, the heart begins to beat.
2. At 40 days, an EEG can detect brain waves.
3. At 6 to 7 weeks, the baby can respond to touch.
4. At 8 weeks, he or she has every required body part.
5. The duration of the pregnancy is for growth of the fully developed body parts.

Though many people consider such concerns off limits, one can't escape thinking about child development. We wonder what our child might have been. We imagine what his or her life might have been like.

God Sees All and Knows All

God knows what our unborn babies were like in every cell of their bodies. He knows what the child would have looked like at 12 years old or as a young adult. Life does not begin with the first breath or the first heartbeat. It begins in the heart and mind of God before conception. Women have been endowed with the incredible ability and opportunity to give life to eternal souls created in the image of God!

As you acknowledge the choice you made to end your baby's life, you feel alone in your thoughts and feelings. Who would understand such dreary thinking? The act of abortion is not openly discussed, so who would allow your mother heart to wander into such wonderings and questions? Even when a woman loses a child to miscarriage or stillbirth, she feels discomfort in such a discussion. How much greater, then, is the secret issue of abortion. I have good news for you, my sister: Someone does understand. Look with me at some other parts of Psalm 139:

> You have searched me, LORD, and you know me.
> You know when I sit and when I rise; you perceive my
>   thoughts from afar.
> You discern my going out and my lying down; you are
>   familiar with all my ways.
> Before a word is on my tongue you, LORD, know it
>   completely.
> You hem me in behind and before, and you lay your hand
>   upon me.
> Such knowledge is too wonderful for me, too lofty for me
>   to attain.
> Where can I go from your Spirit? Where can I flee from
>   your presence?
> If I go up to the heavens, you are there; if I make my bed
>   in the depths, you are there.
> If I rise on the wings of the dawn, if I settle on the far side
>   of the sea,

even there your hand will guide me, your right hand
will hold me fast.
If I say, "Surely the darkness will hide me and the
light become night around me,"
even the darkness will not be dark to you; the
night will shine like the day, for darkness is as
light to you (Psalm 139:1-12, *NIV*).

Nothing is hidden from God's sight. He is with you during the darkest, loneliest and most difficult times of your life. God sees with complete clarity into the darkness of your soul and deep secrets. God never leaves you.

God Forgives and Revives

Many men and women report feelings of guilt, shame, depression, regret and anger over their abortion. Others describe struggling with feelings of unworthiness, fear, numbness and lack of trust. As a result, many turn to substance abuse and other destructive behaviors.

Do some of these emotions or actions sound familiar? Perhaps you have never before connected the dots and realized that your feelings could be a result of your abortion. That's just one more proof that the enemy continually strives to keep us from understanding the cause and effect of post-abortive trauma in women—and men.

In another passage of Scripture, the psalmist wrote, "When I kept silent about my sin, my body wasted away through my groaning all day long. For day and night your hand was heavy upon me; my vitality was drained away as with the fever heat of summer" (Psalm 32.3-4, *NASB*). Praise God, the psalmist didn't describe only the problem! He gives us the healing solution: "I acknowledged my sin to You, and my iniquity I did not hide; I said, 'I will confess my transgressions to the LORD'; and You forgave the guilt of my sin" (Psalm 32:5, *NASB*).

According to this passage, when we stay silent regarding our sin, our bodies waste away and our energy literally drains away. Secrets can play havoc on a person's physical, emotional, mental and spiritual well-being. We can't allow ourselves to stop with the loss. God wants to heal our hearts and use our stories to help others. Confession leads to forgiveness and peace.

God promises hope and redemption to those who come to Him. Other remedies we've tried in an effort to relieve the pain of abortion trap us in dark places. We've tried self-destructive remedies like drugs, alcohol and meaningless relationships. Perhaps you've already discovered that you can't find your way out of the dark places alone.

Rescue begins when you acknowledge that you are powerless to heal your life on your own. Only the Savior can rescue, re-create and restore you from the inside out. If you want to experience healing, you must be willing to trust Jesus to take you on the unfamiliar and risky path that leads there.

Heart to Heart from Pat

The enemy knows where we are vulnerable, and he knows what it will take to set us free. He does not like truth; he does not like freedom.

Jesus' words recorded in John 8:44 (*NIV*) tell us, "[the devil] was a murderer from the beginning, not holding to the truth, for there is no truth in him. When he lies, he speaks his native language, for he is a liar and the father of lies." Just a few verses earlier, Jesus said that when you know the truth, the truth will set you free (see John 8:32). This is God's only reason for drawing you to this study. His purpose is not to shame you, but to cut away the shame from you—to help you see the truth about abortion so that you can get free from its grip on your past.

There was a woman who came to a well where Jesus had gone to rest and get a drink of water. The story is found in John, chapter 4. The woman, who had also come to the well for water, had a life-changing encounter with Jesus when He confronted her secrets. He knew about her past; he knew about the guys and the marriages and the abuse and the load she carried deep in her heart.

We know that Jesus came to the well without burdens because the woman asked Him how He was going to get water without having something to put it in. She, on the other hand, was loaded down with a big heavy jar for her water, and she was loaded down with all the dark secrets of her life.

As you and I take our next step toward the mountain peak, you may feel a lot like the woman who came to the well. She was feeling hot, tired and loaded down with burdens she was very tired of carrying. I know that you have come to this place with a heavy load that our Lord does not want you to carry.

My family has a dirty old hiking backpack we have used for a lot of years. We usually have some things in it that we need for a good long hike—some water, some refreshments and a map! But after a few uses, we begin to gather stuff that makes that backpack heavier, and we need to lighten the load. In many ways, this healing journey is a lot like a mountain climb, mainly because there is a marvelous destination and it is well worth the climb. But you need to take a look inside your "backpack." This chapter gives you the opportunity to dump out some stuff that will slow you down or keep you from getting to the top.

After the woman encountered Jesus at the well, her response to His knowledge of her past failures and shame turned to excitement and a sense of complete freedom. Instead of a slow, heavy walk back to town, she *ran* back, telling people, "He knew me. He knew my sin. He knew my secrets. . . He is the Messiah." Her load was light, her run swift and free! Jesus is your Messiah, and He wants the same freedom for you today as you start this healing journey.

The very first time that I ever told the story of my abortion experience out loud was with my dear friend Ann. I am all too familiar with the panic in your heart right now and the sick feeling in your stomach. You may have been holding on to your secret for 10 years, as I did—or it may even be 20 years. Or maybe you've been holding it for a year! The choice to have an abortion is sold to women as the great escape, the easy out, the quick fix and, sometimes, the only choice.

We know differently, don't we? We know that nothing can compare to the intentional destruction of our own child. No one can ever completely understand the shame and loss we feel. That is, no one but Jesus! How very difficult it is to even speak the words that tell the story. But God wants to help you. The Bible says, "Confess your sins to each other and pray for each other so that you may be healed" (James 5:16, *NIV*). Isn't God amazing? He knows how much we need one another.

God will help you when the time comes to share with the right person or persons. When I shared with my friend Ann, she had not had an abortion in her past. She had never heard an abortion story and had no idea what I was going to share with her; but I can tell you that God Himself filled her heart and her mouth, and she easily and sincerely embraced me and spoke words of love and support and truth to me in those moments. Her godly response changed my life.

I am praying that every person who reads this book and needs a trustworthy someone to share with will find that person. But I can assure you that the Surrendering the Secret leadership team is here for you. Contact us through our website or Facebook and we will help you process your story.

JOURNAL TIME

Spend time in prayer and reflection. Ask God to help you get a deeper insight into all that you have considered in this chapter. You may have encountered a lot of new information. You may never have envisioned aborted children as "being knit together by God." Give God time to show you His heart for you as you proceed toward the complete healing He wants for you. God may show you how you have allowed the enemy's lies to push you around. He also may show you how you have been affected by the lie when faced with it by well-meaning friends, family, the church or the media.

God created us in His image (see Genesis 1:27) with the freedom of choice. Since the moment Adam and Eve chose to disobey God, the world has been anything but paradise. Our freedom to choose has destroyed life across the ages, but God created us with the freedom to make our own decisions. We always have free choice, yet choices always have consequences. Before entering the Promised Land, Moses challenged the Israelites, saying, "Today I have given you the choice between life and death, between blessings and curses. Now I call on heaven and earth to witness the choice you make. Oh, that you would choose life, so that you and your descendants might live!" (Deuteronomy 30:19, *NLT*).

Today, will you reject the past with its shame, curses and death, and choose instead the path to life, freedom and blessing with Jesus? Will you choose life?

This can be an overwhelming chapter for you. You may be reading these truths for the first time. New feelings may be stirring inside you, and you may begin to feel angry. That is to be expected. The next chapter will deal with the emotion of anger as the post-abortive woman manifests it. As you reflect on your journey, let me suggest some clarifying questions to ask yourself. These questions will help you to think through aspects of your situation.

Questions to Consider: Regarding the Father of the Child

1. What part did your relationship with your child's father play in your decision? Was he involved? Did he know about your choice?

2. If you were the father, was the choice made without your input?

3. If you contributed to the choice, do you feel that you had all of the truth when you made your abortion decision?

When you ask God a question, expect His Spirit to respond to your heart. Be careful not to rush it or manufacture an answer. Don't turn the Bible into a reference book or spiritual encyclopedia. Just pose the question to God and wait on Him. The litmus test for anything we hear from God is alignment with the Bible as our ultimate truth source.

The following questions ask you to look into your heart and consider, with brutal honesty, your deepest feelings and beliefs. Remember, your behavior is the best indicator of what you really believe in your innermost being (see Psalm 51:6). Be sure to capture your insights and feelings on these pages or in your journal.

Questions to Consider: Ask Yourself

1. What lies have I held on to that have prevented me from feeling the full impact of my decision to end my child's life?

2. What do I now believe as the truth? Are there any lies remaining?

Questions to Consider: Ask God

1. Your Word says that You can see me, Lord. Why do You allow something like abortion to be available to us when You know how much it will hurt?

2. Why didn't You stop me?

3. Where were You?

Notes

1. Medical and statistical information was taken from the article "Medical Report/Women's Health/Abortion. . . Is There a Connection?" NOEL: noelinfo@noelforlife.org (accessed October 2006). Statistics regarding post-abortion trauma are very difficult to confirm and standardize. I have used the most commonly used information that is available at the time of this writing. I encourage you as a reader to research this information on your own and I truly feel that your heart will be stirred to action as you uncover for yourself the heartbreak of abortion.

2. "Abortion Data" from Reports of the Alan Guttmacher Institute: www.religioustolerance. org/abo_fact3.htm (accessed November 2006).

3. "Medical Report/Women's Health/Abortion. . . Is There a Connection?"

4

Like Drinking Poison ⇐ ⇐ ⇐

Looking into the numbers of people affected by abortion and examining the intentional strategies of abortion proponents causes women to begin to think about other people who might have been involved in their abortion decision. You may be feeling that even reading this book is complicating your life, not making it easier. You've had to draw on immense courage to revisit the past and face some difficult truths. Right about now, you are probably wondering, *Why am I doing this to myself?*

Please don't give up. Keep reading. It is costly to go back, but it is more costly not to go back. Your freedom is worth the cost. Freedom and the truth you will find in your search could save a life and will definitely change yours.

● ● ●

I struggled to open my eyes. Although I could hear soft whispers in the room, I could not move my body or speak past the tube running down my throat. I couldn't remember where I was or how I got there. Within moments, I would wish I had not awakened at all.

My newly wedded husband and my parents were standing numbly at the foot of my hospital bed as I struggled to regain consciousness.

As tiny bits of my body and my mind began to regain feeling, a flood of anger rushed into each space. *Now, I remember.*

The people at the hospital said that the whole procedure would be over in 30 minutes. They said I would be picking up my five-year-old son from school that afternoon. They said a few aspirin would do the trick after the procedure.

Nothing they said was true.

My abortion was supposed to be a three-hour break in my busy day, allowing me to go on with my life by noon. Instead, I had an allergic reaction to the anesthesia they used to put me to sleep and they had to put me on a respirator to keep me alive. By noon, I was still unable to breathe on my own, much less pick up my son from school. My new husband was forced to call on my parents to do that for us. Of course, after picking up our son from school, my parents rushed to the hospital.

The people at the clinic had said no one would even have to know. They said there was "no need to worry" about the fever and the cramps that lasted five days after I went home from the hospital. When the symptoms grew worse, they changed their minds and said, "During the emergency we encountered during your first procedure, parts of the fetus were left behind. We will need to repeat the abortion procedure."

I never even thought about the word "fetus" until they said it. After that, all I could think was "baby." My baby. "Parts" left behind? Which "parts"? The heart? The hands? Parts of a boy, or of a girl? My God, which parts?

Nothing they said was true.

• • •

Facing the truth about abortion means facing the facts about the millions upon millions of people who are affected—who are permanently scarred. Facing the truth forces us to understand how many sisters, friends, aunts, cousins and daughters endure the heartbreak and shame of abortion, and we have to shed the false comfort of believing what we wish were real. When we take the time to understand the truth about abortion, we often feel anger.

Anger is an extremely powerful emotion. Most of the time, we view it as a negative part of ourselves that should be denied or at least tightly controlled. The truth is that God created all of our emotions for our benefit—including the emotion of anger. However, when we don't use emotions properly, we can do a great deal of damage to others and to ourselves. Let's talk about anger—the good, the bad and the ugly.

The Power of Anger

The Bible has much to say about how to handle our emotions the right way. A verse in Ephesians shows us that anger isn't necessarily a sin. It instructs us to lay aside falsehood and "speak the truth each one of you with his neighbor, for we are members of one another. Be angry, and yet do not sin" (Ephesians 4:25-26, *NASB*).

What? Did the Bible just give us permission to be angry? Anger is a God-given emotion and is not a sin. How we deal with our anger may be either wholesome or sinful. Anger becomes dangerous and destructive when we react to it in ways that can hurt others and ourselves.

Think of unmanaged anger as being like the acid in your car battery. In the right container, and used for the right purpose, the acid provides power to start your car. In the wrong container, anger becomes corrosive and destructive of whatever it comes into contact with.

God gave you the ability to feel anger as a motivating force. When we encounter false and hurtful things, anger motivates us to change them. But anger has a short useful shelf life. If we hold on to our anger for weeks, months or years, it can overtake us and consume who we are. As anger corrodes our soul, every thought and every action can become motivated by anger, resulting in bitterness. The person God created us to be ends up buried beneath our anger, with resentment and bitterness piled on top.

The words "be angry" in Ephesians 4:26 are in the Greek imperative tense used for a command or direct instruction. It's a shock to those of us who have learned to deny and stuff our anger that in this passage God actually commands us to be angry. Two excellent examples from the Bible illustrate God's command: the first is in the life of Moses, and the second is in the life of Jesus.

Moses was an Israelite slave in Egypt whom God miraculously spared from slaughter through his mother's great courage and sacrifice. God raised Moses into a position of great influence in Pharaoh's household, but the events of one day changed all that. The book of Exodus tells the story:

> Years later, after Moses had grown up, he went out to his own people and observed their forced labor. He saw an Egyptian beating a Hebrew, one of his people. Looking all around and seeing no one, he struck the Egyptian dead and

hid him in the sand. The next day he went out and saw two Hebrews fighting. He asked the one in the wrong, "Why are you attacking your neighbor?" "Who made you a leader and judge over us?" the man replied. "Are you planning to kill me as you killed the Egyptian?" Then Moses became afraid and thought: What I did is certainly known. When Pharaoh heard about this, he tried to kill Moses. But Moses fled from Pharaoh and went to live in the land of Midian (Exodus 2:11-15).

Moses got angry when he saw how Egyptians were treating the Hebrews—his people. His anger was justified. What was not justified was allowing that anger to spill over into killing the Egyptian. Moses' sin was not in being angry but in committing murder. His response to anger was not healthy or constructive in solving Israel's problem. It actually made things worse and resulted in Moses having to flee the country.

Moses should have and could have channeled his anger in more constructive ways. To illustrate, Fredrick Douglass was a slave in the pre-Civil War South. After escaping slavery, he became an abolitionist leader who, as an author and orator, greatly influenced efforts to outlaw slavery. Douglass channeled his anger in constructive ways. The result contributed to freedom for millions and changed history.

Jesus provides us another example of constructive channeling of anger. When He saw how Temple businessmen were cheating and extorting people who came to the Temple to worship God, Jesus demonstrated anger:

Jesus entered the Temple and began to drive out all the people buying and selling animals for sacrifice. He knocked over the tables of the moneychangers and the chairs of those selling doves. He said to them, "The Scriptures declare, 'My Temple will be called a house of prayer,' but you have turned it into a den of thieves!" (Matthew 21:12-13, *NLT*).

Jesus did not destructively hurt anyone. Yes, He made a mess, but Jesus channeled His anger for a purpose. He was angry at how the people of Jerusalem were treating the Temple. They had turned a holy place into a market, a place where people were taking advantage of others. It was no longer a place of worship; it was a place of business. His actions were instructive and corrective. In the process, He definitely ruffled some feathers and possibly raised a few welts.

Of course, as the Son of God, Jesus was better able to judge the degree of action to take with His anger. I'm not recommending that any of us take a bullwhip to the person in the overpriced kiosk at the mall. The offense Jesus faced was serious. His reaction was measured and in proportion to the offense.

From Jesus' cleansing of the temple we can see that physically expressing anger can be justified under some circumstances. Such righteous anger must be neither a means to selfish gain nor a way to hurt someone. Acting on anger may be justified when it results in a change and makes the world a better place. Godly anger aligns us with the emotion God feels when people are abused.

As post-abortive women, we have to deal with a great amount of anger. The challenge is to sort through that anger and express it in healthy and constructive ways. How we deal with anger will be different for each of us, but it has some common elements.

Unhealthy Ways to Express Anger

When it comes to expressing anger, you may tend to *implode* (hold your anger in) or *explode* (express your anger with aggressive behaviors). Dr. Gary Chapman and Jennifer Thomas, in their book *The Five Languages of Apology*, describe these two unhealthy ways of managing anger.

Internalized Anger

Implosive anger is internalized anger that a person never expresses outwardly. You might hear someone say, "I'm not angry, just frustrated" or "I'm not mad, just disappointed." These are the kind of words spoken by someone who handles anger by imploding.

Because so many of us have been taught to deny our anger, we would do well to examine the previously cited Bible passage from Ephesians a little more closely:

> Therefore, laying aside falsehood, speak truth each one of you with his neighbor, for we are members of one another. Be angry, and yet do not sin; do not let the sun go down on your anger, and do not give the devil an opportunity. He who steals must steal no longer; but rather he must

labor, performing with his own hands what is good, so that he will have something to share with one who has need. Let no unwholesome word proceed from your mouth, but only such a word as is good for edification according to the need of the moment, so that it will give grace to those who hear. Do not grieve the Holy Spirit of God, by whom you were sealed for the day of redemption. Let all bitterness and wrath and anger and clamor and slander be put away from you, along with all malice. Be kind to one another, tender-hearted, forgiving each other, just as God in Christ also has forgiven you (Ephesians 4:25-32, *NASB*).

The apostle Paul tells us that unexpressed, or bottled-up, anger gives the devil an opportunity to influence us, grieves the Holy Spirit and gives bitterness, wrath, anger, clamor, slander and malice a foothold in our lives. In verse 29, the word "unwholesome" means *rotten*. If we allow anger to fester, it will lead to rottenness. Eventually, it will consume all that we do and all that we are. The end product of such stuffed anger is a heart filled with bitterness and unforgiveness.

To be human means that you will experience an occasional bout of anger; but haven't you known someone whose anger has become more than a passing phase? The word "bitter" comes to mind. Think of bitterness as the ossified form of anger. When we don't deal with our anger, it gradually petrifies. If we continue to bury our anger, we risk becoming like a person dragging around the skeleton of a long-dead dinosaur. Unforgiveness weighs us down; it saps our strength and poisons our character.

Implosive anger has to find expression somehow, so when it comes out it takes the form of passive-aggressive behavior, displaced anger, physiological and emotional stress, resentment, bitterness and hatred. Imploders typically keep score, so living with an imploder always carries the potential for a delayed explosion from his or her dormant volcano of anger.

When Paul advised, "Do not let the sun go down on your anger," he wasn't dealing in religious platitudes. He was warning us to deal with our anger promptly and effectively before it can spread and do more damage. He also warned, "Do not give the devil an opportunity." Paul explained that poorly managed anger offers the devil a *topos*—the Greek word from which we get our word "topography"—and it means giving the devil a plot of land.

Imagine that you are fighting a war (you *are* fighting a war, by the way). The very last thing you would want to do is to freely grant your enemy a military base from which to launch more attacks into your life and relationships. When you put anger aside and save it for tomorrow, you grant your enemy that forward-operating base. He will prove more than willing to lob mortar shells at you from the location you've allowed him to occupy.

Implosive anger takes an emotion that God built into each one of us and turns it into a self-destructive internal source of conflict. It can pop up at any time and always in a most unhealthy way. Sometimes we toggle back and forth between imploding and exploding.

Externalized Anger

Explosive anger is the other unhealthy, ungodly management technique. We may manifest it as uncontrolled fury in a verbal and/or physical form. According to Ephesians 4:31, the outcome of all poorly managed anger is bitterness, wrath, more anger, clamor, slander and malice.

Explosive anger verbally attacks by screaming, cursing, condemning, name-calling, humiliating or threatening. It damages the self-esteem of both the exploder and the one being attacked. Ultimately, it destroys relationships, because the exploder causes the anger recipient to retreat for emotional safety. Exploders frequently blame their victims for "making them mad" or they minimize their outbursts by labeling them "blowing off steam." In extreme cases, the exploder may grab, push or strike in anger. All unhealthy anger is harmful, but physical abuse should never be tolerated.

Toward a Healthy Alternative

Like water in a leaky container, unresolved anger never remains confined. It always finds some unhealthy way to express itself. Gary Chapman and Jennifer Thomas, in their book *The Five Languages of Apology,* wrote, "When one's sense of right is violated, that person will experience anger. He or she will feel wronged and resentful at the person [or persons] who has violated their trust."[1]

Post-abortive women often react to things in ways they don't understand. They may overreact to events and circumstances in ways they wouldn't have expected—sometimes with anger or with great sadness or hurt. Now that you are on your healing journey, you can begin to make sense of these uncomfortable emotions.

Common circumstances can trigger anger for post-abortive women. All of these things and events have the potential to push your anger button: baby showers, mothers with their children, books about fetal development, doctor visits, certain smells or odors, literature related to abortion, pregnant women, being around a hospital nursery and birth event. Videos and TV programs related to pregnancy and birth, pro-life/pro-choice advertisements and commercials add to the inner turmoil. Every woman describes different responses to these triggers: A specific sound or odor may cause nausea; baby showers may generate feelings of dread; you may avoid friends or family members who have children. Some women may become avid about pro-life or even pro-choice arguments as a way to deal with their abortion decision.

When you come face-to-face with your abortion decision, you will be reminded of people who were involved in that choice. In reflecting on these people and their influence, you are reminded of the confusion, the pressure and perhaps the feeling that you had no other choice. As a result, you may aim your post-abortion anger at a variety of targets. You may not even feel anger toward these targets, but rather your anger comes across as feelings of responsibility.

Potential targets for your anger may include: those who withheld the truth about abortion; friends who presented abortion as the best choice; yourself, for allowing the unplanned pregnancy; doctors and nurses; extended family members; teachers or school counselors; church or religious leaders; the father of the baby; parents; God; the abortion clinic; the baby; the media; and even the lawmakers.

We often hesitate to admit our anger toward others for fear of rejection. We find ourselves defending those we feel we should love. But in order to heal, it's important to acknowledge anger and release it in a healthy way.

Ephesians Anger Checklist

The following numbered list, based on experience and the Ephesians passage, is to help you evaluate and deal with anger issues. Consider your responses in each of these areas:

1. *Assess your primary emotion:* Does my anger stem from loss of control, hurt or indignation about wrongs?
2. *Take off your mask:* What has hurt you? Talk through your feelings (see Ephesians 4:25).
3. *Deal with issues and confront:* Have you learned to communicate issues clearly and early? Be sure the goal is resolving issues, not getting back at people (see Ephesians 4:26-27).
4. *Don't let anger fester and rot:* Are you harboring unresolved anger? Buried anger scribbles a written invitation to the enemy to exploit us in wounding others and ourselves (see Ephesians 4:29).
5. *God cares deeply about your anger:* Ask yourself, *Have I turned my anger over to God?* His heart aches when we allow rage, resentment or bitterness to take root and grow (see Ephesians 4:30-31).
6. *Replace anger with forgiveness and compassion:* Have you received the forgiveness God offers? Have you extended that forgiveness to others? Because God has forgiven us so much, we need to be willing to forgive others (see Ephesians 4:32).

Heart to Heart from Pat

By now you have figured out that I am a pretty transparent person. You and I have made lots of confessions on this journey together so far. One of my first confessions to you was that I am not an overly athletic person, and that is true; however, I am a person who deeply loves the outdoors and God's creation in nature. I love the crystal-clear Gulf beaches that are minutes from my doorstep; I love snow-covered mountain peaks; and I have loved, since my childhood, hiking in the tree-covered Blue Ridge Mountains. I love the smell of the crisp morning air, the deep, thick green of the trees, and the cool rumbling of mountain streams that always appear to be flowing up the mountain to me.

Since I am an amateur hiker at best, I always obey the warning signs. If a sign says, "stay on the path," I stay on the path. If it says, "falling rocks," I keep my head on alert; and when a sign says, "do not feed the bears," I choose another path!! God has built some warning signs into our lives to protect us from taking a wrong path or staying on it, and to help us define certain boundaries. Anger is an emotion God gave us that when used correctly has the right result, but when used in the wrong way, leads to death.

I recently read a book about what steals the joy God desires for us. Anger is at the top of the list. We have studied several examples of the truth from our Bible study this past week. In the case of abortion, there are many areas that should cause anger in you and in God's people in general. We should be angry that women are lied to by doctors and medical professionals trusted to protect human life. We should be angry that women are pressured to have abortions by employers and educational institutions and inconvenienced social agencies. We should be angry that teenage girls are drawn in by bold marketing ads placed by abortionists in high school newspapers telling them "no one has to know." However, we have learned through our study that anger that does not lead to healthy responses and positive actions only leads to self-destruction and increased pain and loss.

For your Journal Time, I am going to ask you to write some letters to some of the people who were involved in your abortion decision. It may have been a boyfriend, a parent or possibly one of those professionals I've mentioned. *Don't forget: These letters are not to be mailed!* I pray that just the writing of the letters helps you to understand how many people and circumstances actually played a part in your choice to abort. As alone as you may have felt walking into that abortion clinic, you were not alone in your decision. I pray that you have taken this opportunity to place some blame on other people besides you for a change; you have a right to do that.

This exercise is meant to provide some safe boundaries and a safe place for you to identify and express your anger. Possibly, you have needed this time just to recognize that other people did play a part in your choice. You have been given some warning signs about your emotions that will keep you on the right path so that your anger results in something positive—something that will make a difference for the kingdom of God and be something that will help heal your heart and release any strongholds that have been left in your life as a result of your abortion. Ephesians 4:26 says, "Be angry, but sin not." Spend some time allowing God to show you the way to freedom through those verses in Ephesians 4:25-32.

This process is going to be another "weight loss" session. You are going to lighten your backpack a good bit, and from this point on you are going to begin to see a little bit more of the view. We are getting higher in our climb and, as a matter of fact, after this session, you will be halfway there! Take advantage of this time and this opportunity. It is safe, God planned it for you and it will help you get to your goal. I am continuing to pray for you.

Journal Time

Spend some time reviewing the six steps of the Ephesians anger checklist from this chapter and write your responses. Write the steps and add your own name into the verses as appropriate. Ask God to show you any places of unidentified or unresolved anger from your past. Take some time to write a letter to each person you have identified as someone you are or maybe *should* be angry with who was involved in your abortion experience. After you are done, pray those words of Scripture over those letters; then take the letters somewhere safe and burn them or rip them to pieces as a symbol of surrendering them to God. Close your time in prayer, thanking God for the freedom that is found in forgiveness.

_____

_____

_____

_____

_____

_____

_____

_____

_____

_____

_____

Note

1. Gary Chapman and Jennifer Thomas, *The Five Languages of Apology* (Chicago, IL: Northfield Publishing, 2006), p. 18.

Forgiveness: The Golden Key to Freedom

The process of working through anger can be exhausting. The next part of the journey to freedom is to release the anger and lighten the load of this heavy burden you've been carrying. The goal of this chapter is to start you moving away from anger and toward forgiveness.

As you begin to let go of your anger, think of it as choosing health. Put the burden of resentment in God's hands. Recovery groups have long said that holding on to anger and unforgiveness is like drinking poison and waiting for someone else to die from its effects. In the previous chapter, you took a look at the truth about abortion—its physical, spiritual and emotional aspects. To become angry about abortion is a normal response as you look at what the "free choice" for abortion is truly doing to our sisters, friends, daughters and grandchildren.

As we saw in the last chapter, anger can be good. It can get things done. Anger can get our attention and result in action. One caveat: The energy anger generates must be channeled and directed. Untamed anger lashes out at random. We must learn and discipline ourselves to guide anger's reactive energy to helpful ends. Then the results can include change and restoration. Before you can express anger as a positive emotion, you will look at the healing that comes from not only letting go of your damaging anger, but also look at forgiving those who have hurt you.

In chapter 4, we looked at the people involved in your abortion. Those people may have included the father of the child, nurses, doctors, parents, employer, school personnel, a pastor or church leaders, a counselor and one or more friends. You may find yourself saying, "I want to stop being angry but I just can't."

If you truly want to stop being angry, I must point you to an initially unwanted reality. To experience true healing, you have to make a decision to let go of your anger. The truth is, God wants you to go a step further: He wants you to forgive. In any area of your life where you have been so hurt, it's difficult to imagine forgiving an offender. However, with God's grace, it is possible.

How Can I Possibly Forgive?

In referring to His people, God says, "I will forgive their wickedness and will remember their sins no more" (Jeremiah 31:34b, *NIV*). According to Jeremiah, God forgives us completely. Right now, you may be thinking, *Well, maybe God can forgive completely, but I can't*. Before we can define what genuine forgiveness is and make a case for its necessity in healing, first we need to clarify what forgiveness is not.

Forgiveness is *not* forgetting. We frequently hear the phrase "forgive and forget," but forgiveness does not imply amnesia. When the Bible says that God "will remember their sins no more," it doesn't mean that He suddenly has no recollection of an offense. God does not develop a kind of heavenly Alzheimer's. It means that God chooses not to catalog our sins and use the information against us. God chooses to pass over His right to hold our wrongs against us.

Forgiveness is *not* minimizing the hurt. Forgiveness does not water down the offense by saying something like, "It's okay, it wasn't that bad." Or "I know you didn't mean to hurt me." The truth is, you have been hurt deeply and, sometimes, very intentionally. Forgiveness does not say, "I'm all right; it's just a flesh wound" when real trauma is involved. Instead, forgiveness calls the violation what it is, just as an umpire calls what he sees.

Forgiveness does *not* necessarily mean reconciliation. Perhaps you were thinking, *If I forgive the doctor, my ex-boyfriend and my parents, then I have to initiate or at least be receptive to reconciliation.* Hear this truth: Forgiveness and reconciliation are two separate issues. Keep them apart. You definitely need to forgive, for many reasons. But you choose to reconcile or not to reconcile—and to what degree you reconcile—based on the facts of your situation.

Perhaps you are open to reconciliation and would give anything for it to happen, but reconciliation isn't even on the radar screen of some of the people involved in your abortion. Some people are unsafe for you, and you most definitely should keep your distance from them. In some cases, the very thought of required reconciliation feels like being sentenced to life in prison without parole. Forgiveness recognizes that reconciliation may be neither possible nor wise following the abortion.

Reconciling a relationship is also a matter of degree. Forgiving someone doesn't require becoming best friends or even close acquaintances with him or her. In some cases, you can genuinely forgive without ever initiating a relationship. In other cases, you may reconcile a relationship while maintaining your distance for any number of reasons. It's possible that you may find great love and support through reconciliation.

Have any of these concepts or definitions altered your view of forgiveness? You may find yourself more open to forgive those involved in your abortion when you dispense with wrong concepts of forgiveness.

Joseph's Redemptive Story

The Bible tells a wonderful story about a young man who had every reason to hate and hold a grudge. He even had a delicious opportunity to experience the joy of a "payback," but he chose a different response. Joseph's story begins in Genesis 37, and it goes on for 10 chapters. You may want to take time to read the story in its entirety before continuing to let God show you the way to find redemptive healing.

Joseph was favored by his father but alienated from his brothers. When he was only 17, his brothers plotted to kill him, but then tempered their actions by selling him into slavery. Thus, he found himself a slave in the foreign kingdom of Egypt.

After years spent as a slave, Joseph was imprisoned for a crime he didn't commit. For 13 years he faced shame and rejection. Through a series of divine interventions, Joseph left prison and became the second ruler of Egypt, reporting directly to Pharaoh. Ironically, he found himself facing the very brothers who wronged him, with them in great need of his help.

To add to the drama, Joseph framed his brothers as thieves, but they did not recognize Joseph when they were brought before him.

Joseph held in his hands the very thing for which bitter people everywhere long: He had all the power. Joseph could pay his brothers back. Unlimited revenge was within his grasp. His brothers didn't even know that Joseph could understand their language as they whispered together. With the brothers trembling in fear, Joseph. . . well, read the account directly from Genesis 45:

> Joseph could no longer keep his composure in front of all his attendants, so he called out, "Send everyone away from me!" No one was with him when he revealed his identity to his brothers. But he wept so loudly that the Egyptians heard it, and also Pharaoh's household heard it. Joseph said to his brothers, "I am Joseph! Is my father still living?" But they could not answer him because they were terrified in his presence. Then Joseph said to his brothers, "Please, come near me," and they came near. "I am Joseph, your brother," he said, "the one you sold into Egypt. And now don't be worried or angry with yourselves for selling me here, because God sent me ahead of you to preserve life. For the famine has been in the land these two years, and there will be five more years without plowing or harvesting. God sent me ahead of you to establish you as a remnant within the land and to keep you alive by a great deliverance. Therefore it was not you who sent me here, but God. He has made me a father to Pharaoh, lord of his entire household, and ruler over all the land of Egypt" (Genesis 45:1-8).

When Joseph's brothers recognized him, they were terrified. They had sold him into slavery years before. They never imagined that he would be second in command in Egypt. For all they knew, he was dead.

Joseph's perspective about God enabled him to forgive his brothers. He saw God's hand in everything that had happened. Being sold into slavery had resulted in his chance to save the lives of his father and his brothers.

Joseph had every reason and opportunity to repay his brothers for the agony they caused him. Joseph, however, did not choose to take that opportunity. He forgave them because he'd allowed love to replace bitterness, and because he'd learned the truth the apostle Paul later expressed in Romans 8:28. Joseph understood that "God causes all things to work together for good to those who love God, to those who are called according to His purpose" (Romans 8:28, *NASB*).

The whole of the New Testament further enforces the need to forgive. But let's take one story to illustrate. A man came to Jesus and asked how many times he had to forgive his brother. Matthew 18 records Jesus' response. Jesus described a man who owed a vast amount of money. The holder of his debt decided to have the man and his entire family thrown in a debtor's prison, but the man begged for leniency. The master forgave the man his massive debt, but the man promptly accosted another man who owed him a small debt. When the master heard what the forgiven debtor had done, he summoned him and said, "You wicked slave! I forgave you all that debt because you begged me. Shouldn't you also have had mercy on your fellow slave, as I had mercy on you?" (Matthew 18:32-33).

As the consummate rabbi, Jesus knew that the most powerful way to teach is to lay out the truth but allow the hearers to make the connections for themselves. In the story of the debtor, the underlying question is, how can we be so petty as to refuse to forgive the relatively small debt of what others have done to us when God has forgiven us the massive wrong of our sin debt? If even the most sinned-against among us were to pile up all the wrongs they have endured, could the list ever compare to what the perfect and totally innocent Son of God endured?

God requires us to forgive those who offend us. He does not give us the option to choose whom we'll forgive and against whom we will continue to hold a grudge. Paul wrote, "Make allowance for each other's faults, and forgive anyone who offends you. Remember, the Lord forgave you, so you must forgive others" (Colossians 3:13, *NLT*).

God commands us to forgive—for His glory, for the healing of others and for our own benefit. Forgiveness helps maintain harmony in relationships and creates deep peace and joy in the lives of the two captives it sets free—your offender *and* you!

As a woman who has faced the pain and loneliness of abortion, you have a reason to be angry with many people—at the very least, the lawmakers, the media and the medical community that has betrayed their responsibility to protect life and to ensure truth. You have reason to be angry and to feel cheated by some of your loved ones and your circumstances.

True forgiveness is seldom easy. It can be quite costly. But it offers you a powerful weapon for tearing down strongholds in your heart and resultant negative patterns of living. The enemy uses unforgiveness and anger to keep you in bondage. When you surrender your unforgiveness and anger, you set your own heart free so that God can take you places you never dreamed possible.

Barriers to Forgiveness

A number of barriers can hinder a person from letting go of anger and interfere in the healing process. Here are a few examples:

- If I forgive the offender, he/she will never understand the severity of the offense.
- If I forgive, I will look weak. I have my pride.
- He/she doesn't deserve forgiveness, only punishment. I can't let him/her off the hook.
- Forgiveness isn't possible for this circumstance. I believe that abortion is unforgivable.
- The offender shows no remorse, so I have no responsibility to forgive.
- If I let go of my anger, I may also let go of my child.
- Letting go of anger means letting go of my relationship with persons involved in the abortion. (Sometimes anger is the only emotion connecting people.)
- I'm comfortable with the status quo, and I'm afraid of the unknowns that will come.

Get Out of Prison

We often believe the lie that our anger effectively punishes the offender. The truth is that we are the only ones undergoing punishment and imprisonment by holding on to anger. In his book *Wishful Thinking,* Frederick Buechner wrote:

Of the Seven Deadly Sins, anger is possibly the most fun. To lick your wounds, to smack your lips over grievances long past, to roll over your tongues the prospect of bitter confrontations still to come, to savor to the last toothsome morsel both the pain you are given and the pain you are giving back—in many ways it is a feast fit for a king. The chief drawback is that what you are wolfing down is yourself. The skeleton at the feast is you. When we choose to forgive, we release our prisoner from the dungeon and discover that we are subsequently freed from the dank cell of our own bitterness. Spiritually and emotionally, forgiveness frees us.[1]

In Genesis 50:20, Joseph told his brothers, "You intended to harm me, but God intended it for good to accomplish what is now being done, the saving of many lives" (*NIV*). You may not even imagine being able to say these words. But keep letting God do His work in you.

Forgiving Others and Accepting Forgiveness

We post-abortive women commonly feel that while God has forgiven us, we cannot seem to forgive ourselves. It's important to grasp a crucial truth that may surprise you. Although our self-help culture talks about the need to forgive ourselves, God never intended for us to do that. The Bible does not identify the need to forgive ourselves. In fact, I don't think we are capable of it.

The key is to accept God's forgiveness. When we try to forgive ourselves, we seek to do God's work in His place. This distinction may trouble you and seem like semantics, but it goes to the very heart of the Scriptures and the gospel. Let me try to explain with two biblical examples.

In the Garden of Eden, God gave our first human parents a division of labor—not between Adam and Eve but between the pair and God. They were to take care of the tasks God gave them: tend the garden; populate the earth—that sort of human stuff. God was to take care of the God stuff. But in Genesis 3, Satan came and tempted Eve with the thought that God was holding out on them. If they would just disobey God and make their own decisions (eat the fruit), they would become "like God, knowing good and evil."

For millennia, theologians have debated and tried to describe the heart of Eve and Adam's sin. They use the word "pride" or other terms, but this is certain: Eve wanted to have what God had and to take over His place.

What does that have to do with forgiving? In the same way that forgiving is God's territory, not ours. Only He is holy. All sin may hurt us, but it is ultimately an offense against Him. Only He has the infinite power to forgive. When we push Him aside like a petulant preschooler and say, "Me do it," we only interfere with the process.

Allow me a second biblical illustration from the gospel. The gospel is the good news that Christ died for our sins to do for us what we could never do for ourselves. The gospel means much more than simply forgiveness, but it certainly means no less. Ephesians 2 underscores the glorious fact that the gospel is a gift: "For you are saved by grace through faith, and this is not from yourselves; it is God's gift—not from works, so that no one can boast" (Ephesians 2:8-9).

What would happen if someone were to say, "I would rather do it myself. I don't have to rely on God's gift (though it cost the Son of God's death). I choose to do it myself"? The question is not hypothetical, for people reject the gospel every day and choose to "do it themselves." In the words of Dr. Phil, "How's that working out?"

Please don't miss this application in either of these two ways. First, don't miss the giant cosmic application. If you have been trying to justify yourself, even the tiniest bit, stop it! Recognize that you cannot be good enough for God. Stop trying to make yourself pleasing and accept the reality that Christ's death for us presents us as a perfect offering to God. As a friend says, "If Jesus' death on the cross didn't make God happy [big theological word: "propitiation" for sin], then nothing you do is going to make Him happy."

Also, don't miss the smaller but critically important application: You can't forgive you. That's God's job. His forgiveness is a gift. Accept it.

Having said that, we need to come back and say that accepting forgiveness for yourself and living with the reality that you are forgiven are absolutely essential. You don't need to be forgiven over and over for the same sin. You do, however, need to dip yourself again and again in the reality that if you are in Christ, you are a new creation.

Heart to Heart from Pat

Many years ago, I found myself at a place in life that was not what every little girl dreams of. I was wallowing in the ugly results of lots of bad choices. My marriage was in shambles; my two young sons were living in a very bad family environment that was going nowhere fast.

My life was falling apart, and I had no idea how to fix it. I had actually spent several years and several thousand dollars with a secular therapist who told me to dump my husband and my kids and find myself. Thank the Lord I had enough of Him in me from my childhood that I knew that was not my answer.

Because I didn't know what else to do, I went to church. I was deeply in shame and guilt, and I was so afraid of anyone finding out who I really was. At the same time, I was desperate for a change in my life.

After a few months of hiding out in the Sunday school rooms with my two sons because I was too afraid to go to "big church," a beautiful young woman named Terri invited me to come with her to a weekend ladies' retreat. The topic of the retreat, I later discovered, was anger. I was not aware of any anger in my life; I was aware of lots of bad things, but not anger, or so I thought. I agreed to go with her, and that was when I surrendered my life to Christ. I turned my heart over to Him—fully, completely and passionately. When I rushed to the altar that day at the speaker's invitation, my life was a mess. I had nothing to offer the Lord but my broken heart.

It was many, many years later before that message on anger really sunk in. I pray that over the course of working through the previous few chapters, you have grasped a better understanding of the many ways unresolved anger can show up in your life and become a stronghold for the enemy to keep you trapped without your even knowing it. During your Journal Time, you will be given an opportunity to decide, and declare, that anger and unforgiveness will hold you back no longer.

So far on this journey, we have had some heavy loads to carry, some thirst to overcome, and it has probably felt like a few mountain lions to slay! It is time to clear some paths so that we can get a peak at the view.

I have used my family's hiking backpack as a visual reminder of the burden caused by carrying unhealthy and ungodly behaviors and emotions on your journey with God. We have lightened it a bit each week with the junk God wants you to dump off and leave behind— secrets, lies and anger. In the *Amplified Bible*, Hebrews 12:1 says that we are instructed to "strip off and throw aside every encumbrance (unnecessary weight) and that sin which so readily (deftly and cleverly) clings to and entangles us." Can't you just picture that entanglement in your life? The rest of the Scripture says that we are to press on "with patient endurance and steady and active persistence the appointed race" or journey that God has planned for us.

Mark 11:25 says, "And whenever you stand praying, if you have anything against anyone, forgive him and let it drop (leave it, let it go), in order that your Father who in Heaven may also forgive you your [own] failings and shortcoming and let them drop" (*AMP*). I cannot speak for you, but I want my failings and shortcomings to be dropped by those who have charges against me! Early in my walk with God, I began to change my focus from the failures and abuses that I had received from others, and to look upon my own sins and failures. It is such a difficult process but always clears the path to walk straight into the arms of our Lord.

In this chapter, you have learned about getting some things out of your way that have been blocking your walk with the Lord. We have looked at what forgiveness is and what it is not. True forgiveness is not a feeling; rather, it is a choice for life and not for death. Forgiveness is an act of obedience to God and an act of surrender that will allow His full blessing on your life as you release the entanglement of holding on to unforgiveness. When you forgive a person, he or she is permanently forgiven. When Satan tries to drag you back down and make you think that you haven't really forgiven someone, just speak right back at him the words of truth that you have captured this week.

We are to forgive the same way that God forgives—supernaturally, permanently and unconditionally. This is going to be an amazing session, one that I truly feel you will never forget.

In my home, I have a special place where I meet God. It is a big, fluffy, overstuffed green chair in my living room. It has been reupholstered many times. I call it my prayer chair. I have a basket next to my chair with my reading glasses, a few different Bibles, my journal and some pens and highlighters. When I go to my prayer chair, I do whatever Bible study I am currently working on and I have at my fingertips a few prayer books, such as *Praying God's Word* by Beth Moore and one called *Prayers that Avail Much*.

As you step out into this life-changing work of forgiveness, I would like to pray for you again. It is a prayer that I have prayed for myself many times when I have been faced with a person or situation that calls for me to release anger and seek what God has for me to hear and learn.

Father, in the name of Jesus, we make fresh commitment to You to live in peace and harmony, not only with brothers and sisters in the Body of Christ, but also with our friends, associates, neighbors and family and, yes, Lord, even our enemies. We let go of all bitterness, resentment, envy, strife and unkindness in any form. We give no place to the devil, in Jesus' name. Now, Father, my sisters and I ask Your forgiveness. By faith, we receive it, having assurance that we are cleansed from all unrighteousness through Jesus Christ. We ask You to forgive and release all who have wronged and hurt us. Together, we forgive and release them. Deal with them in Your mercy, Lord, and loving-kindness, as we would have You deal with us. From this moment on, we purpose to walk in love, to seek peace, to live in agreement and to conduct ourselves in a manner that is pleasing to You. We know that we have right standing with You, Lord, and that You are attentive to our prayers. It is written in Your Word that Your love has been poured into our hearts by Your Holy Spirit. We desire to be filled with Your righteousness, which brings glory and honor to You. Amen, so be it!

JOURNAL TIME

I suggest that you write Scripture on cards to read and memorize. Here are just a few suggestions; the Bible is absolutely full of affirmations of God's forgiveness. That's what the gospel is all about.

He has rescued us from the domain of darkness and transferred us into the kingdom of the Son He loves. We have redemption, the forgiveness of sins, in Him (Colossians 1:13-14).

In him we have redemption through his blood, the forgiveness of sins, in accordance with the riches of God's grace (Ephesians 1:7, *NIV*).

If we confess our sins, [God] is faithful and righteous to forgive us our sins and to cleanse us from all unrighteousness (1 John 1:9).

God is the One who saves us, forgives us and redeems our sin. Forgiving ourselves does not achieve forgiveness from our sin. According to both passages in Ephesians, we cannot do anything to earn forgiveness; rather, it is a gift of God's grace. Only God can forgive our sins against Him, but we have to confess them. Confession is the only requirement.

When we, as Christ-followers, say, "I know that God can forgive me, but I can't forgive myself," we are elevating our ability to forgive and seeking to take on ourselves God's ability. True healing and freedom only occur when we can accept the forgiveness God so graciously wants to give each of us.

When we do not completely accept God's forgiveness, we are essentially buying the lie that Christ's sacrifice on the cross was not sufficient to cover abortion. How sweet the reality that if we confess our sins, wounds, failures and false beliefs to God, He'll forgive, renew, transform, restore and redeem us.

Note

1. Frederick Buechner, *Wishful Thinking: A Theological ABC* (New York: Harper & Row, 1973), p. 2.

⇨ ⇨ ⇨   The Great Exchange

I felt as if the tears that welled up from the depths of my soul would never stop. That night of sobbing in the bathtub was a major turning point for me. The truth of what I had done to my child had finally sunk into my heart, and my grief overwhelmed me. Abortion had taken so much from me! I grieved over my sinful choices, for the struggles in my life, for my wounded heart, and, most of all, for my precious baby.

After 33 years of carrying the burden myself, I finally gave my sin to God. I thought I'd already done that at the ladies' retreat, but I'd stopped short. Abortion was the last thing on my mind that day. What I had given to God at the altar was my broken life—my marriage, my emotions, my needs and my expectations. I gave what I knew to give. The night in the bathtub, however, I faced the cross. For the first time, I understood the sin that Jesus had personally carried to the cross for me. I understood the darkness of my heart at a level far beyond my personal needs. I understood that I could not save myself, that I needed a Rescuer. Not until that night did I grasp the amazing depth of my Rescuer's love for me.

As I cried, I washed as though I could wash away all the dirt and pain of my life. In truth, I scrubbed at my body the way a rape victim tries to wash away the violent invasion of rape. I had finally grasped the meaning of the cross at a deeper level and gratefully accepted the sacrifice of the cross. I understood that Jesus Christ willingly gave His life for mine—to set me free, to heal me, and to redeem my entire life.

Gradually, the tears for my own loss transformed into tears for the incredible burden Jesus took on Himself and the passionate love that drove Him to shoulder it. My own burden was more than I could bear, but He bore the burdens of every person on the planet.

I began the night releasing tears, but I ended it by releasing my grip on my sins, my hurts and my burdens. A year earlier, at the ladies' retreat, I surrendered my head. That night in the bathtub, I surrendered my heart. The cleansing I felt was amazing! It was wonderful! And it still is.

In the previous chapter, you made great progress in your journey toward forgiving those involved in your abortions. You also began to understand and accept God's forgiveness. The path of forgiveness is intertwined with the path of grieving. As your losses from abortion become more real to you, you will grieve more deeply, and in that grief, you'll need to revisit the step of forgiveness.

As we move together to step 6 on our map, we'll focus on the importance of grieving the losses and receiving God's gift of wholeness.

Two Kinds of Sorrow

Any traumatic event will create sorrow. In the trauma of abortion, many women (and men) experience deep sorrow that leads to depression, addictions and a host of other dark places of the soul.

Grieving does not, however, have to be destructive. God gave us the gift of grieving as a way to deal with life's difficulties and disappointments. The apostle Paul explains the difference between two kinds of sorrow in his second letter to the Corinthian church. He actually said he was glad the Corinthians were experiencing sorrow.

> Now I'm glad—not that you were upset, but that you were jarred into turning things around. You let the distress bring you to God, not drive you from him. The result was all gain, no loss. Distress that drives us to God. . . turns us around. It gets us back in the way of salvation. We never regret that kind of pain. But those who let distress drive them away from God are full of regrets, end up on a deathbed of regrets. And now, isn't it wonderful all the ways in which this distress has goaded you closer to God? You're more alive, more concerned, more sensitive, more reverent, more human, more passionate, more responsible. Looked at from any angle, you've come out of this with purity of heart (2 Corinthians 7:9-11, *THE MESSAGE*).

Paul differentiates between godly distress/sorrow and destructive distress/sorrow. Godly sorrow causes someone to turn back to God. It leads to repentance and never causes regret. On the other hand, destructive sorrow drives people away from God and does cause regret.

In past chapters, we discovered the importance of replacing lies—the false beliefs we've embraced—with truth from God. If we'll allow our pain and sorrow to drive us toward God, rather than away from Him, we'll experience transformation, healing and new life.

Because past memories, sorrows and hurts are uncomfortable, we try to avoid them or find ways to escape the pain. And yet, Paul was happy about the Corinthians' struggles and distress because it jarred them into change. Jesus also promoted godly sorrow and gave those who are hurting a wonderful promise:

> Those who mourn are blessed, for they will be comforted (Matthew 5:4).

Jesus promises comfort to those who mourn. Remembering our losses and grieving them is vital to the healing process. It allows us to remember where we have come from and how God has worked in those circumstances.

Your Trustworthy Guide

As you are truly open about your feelings with God, He'll take you further down the path to healing.

Most of us, though, have doubts about God's goodness and, specifically, about His heart toward us personally. Let's see what God says about us:

> Do not be afraid, for I have ransomed you. I have called you by name; you are mine. When you go through deep waters, I will be with you. When you go through rivers of difficulty, you will not drown. When you walk through the fire of oppression, you will not be burned up; the flames will not consume you. For I am the LORD, your God, the Holy One of Israel, your Savior (Isaiah 43:1-3, *NLT*).

> On that day you, Jerusalem, will not be put to shame for all the wrongs you have done to me, because I will remove from

you your arrogant boasters. Never again will you be haughty on my holy hill. But I will leave within you the meek and humble. The remnant of Israel will trust in the name of the LORD. . . The LORD has taken away your punishment, he has turned back your enemy. The LORD, the King of Israel, is with you; never again will you fear any harm. . . . The LORD your God is with you, the Mighty Warrior who saves. He will take great delight in you; in his love he will no longer rebuke you, but will rejoice over you with singing (Zephaniah 3:11-12,15,17, *NIV*).

God gave Isaiah several assurances when he faced various fears. He promised to be with Isaiah. Difficulties would not drown him; oppression would not burn him; flames of oppression would not consume him.

God promises that He will not put His children to shame (see Zephaniah 3:11) and that He will take away our punishment (see Zephaniah 3:15). However, God does require us to embrace some vital heart attitudes. He wants us to be meek, humble and trusting.

Zephaniah 3:17 tells us that God takes delight in us and rejoices over us. Doesn't that provide you great comfort?

What keeps us from meaningful life change? Fear is often our greatest enemy. We long to return to what is familiar rather than take risks and face the unknown. More than anything else, your healing journey requires that you trust God. Healing the wounds in your innermost being will lead you down paths you never could have imagined. So take one day and one step at a time as you walk into the shadows with Jesus. He will turn the shadows to light, ease your pain and lead you into freedom, truth and the desires of your heart.

We have focused on the vital step of grieving our losses. The next step in the journey will open your mind and heart to the incredible vistas that await you at the summit of your climb. You can become more than you've been and more than you realize. It's time to make the great exchange—to accept who you really are in Christ.

Change from the Inside Out

God's forgiveness, which comes with your confession, is a very powerful force in your life. God's blessings don't stop when you receive salvation. He wants to help you really change. That happens through your repentance. Unfortunately, that word has been given a bad connotation over the years. "Repent" comes from the Greek word *metanoia*, which means to change (*meta*) your mind or understanding (*noia*). The word "metamorphosis" is a related term, meaning a change in form or substance, and is used to describe what occurs when a caterpillar retreats into its cocoon to emerge as a butterfly. This is a wondrous thing in the physical world, but God does even more wondrous things for His children.

> Pay attention, O Jacob, for you are my servant, O Israel. I, the LORD, made you, and I will not forget you. I have swept away your sins like a cloud. I have scattered your offenses like the morning mist. Oh, return to me, for I have paid the price to set you free. Sing, O heavens, for the LORD has done this wondrous thing. Shout for joy, O depths of the earth! Break into song, O mountains and forests and every tree! For the LORD has redeemed Jacob and is glorified in Israel (Isaiah 44:21-23, *NLT*).

God's words in Isaiah 44 apply to the history of Israel, but they also give us an excellent starting place for our repentance. According to verses 21-22, God will not only *not* forget each one of us, but He will also sweep away our sins. He scatters them like the mist, and He has paid the price of our freedom.

Romans 12:1-2 and John 8:31-32 clarify further by separating the process of repentance, or transformation, into God's part and our part:

> I urge you, brothers and sisters, in view of God's mercy, to offer your bodies as a living sacrifice, holy and pleasing to God—this is your true and proper worship. Do not conform to the pattern of this world, but be transformed by the renewing of your mind. Then you will be able to test and approve what God's will is—His good, pleasing and perfect will (Romans 12:1-2, *NIV*).

> Jesus said. . . "If you continue in My word, you really are My disciples. You will know the truth, and the truth will set you free" (John 8:31-32).

God doesn't expect you to change your own life. He asks that you make yourself available to His Holy Spirit by remaining in His presence. As you turn to God and begin to give Him your secrets, your shame, your false beliefs and distorted perspectives, you become engaged in a battle of the mind and heart. Recall the model we discussed in chapter 2 in which our wounds become infected with lies that lead to destructive agreements and a false sense of self.

> For though we live in the world, we do not wage war as the world does. The weapons we fight with are not the weapons of the world. On the contrary, they have divine power to demolish strongholds. We demolish arguments and every pretension that sets itself up against the knowledge of God, and we take captive every thought to make it obedient to Christ (2 Corinthians 10:3-5, *NIV*).

The cosmic battle between good and evil is not waged on the earth. It occurs in a realm we cannot see or even really understand. We must demolish the strongholds that set themselves up against God. We don't use the word "stronghold" very often today. Imagine a castle, fortress or even a battle scene from a movie like *Braveheart* or *Lord of the Rings*. Strongholds are enemy fortresses built in our territory that are made of lies we have allowed to take root. Anything that is contrary to God and His Word can become an enemy foothold that becomes a stronghold.

Destroying these strongholds of falsehood takes a lot of time, muscle and energy. I imagine massive armies attacking and using weapons such as cannons and explosives to crumble these structures to the ground.

As we recognize the battle being waged over our minds and hearts, we begin to understand why change must occur from the inside out. God must do the work in our innermost being—our hearts and minds. He is the One who transforms us. Our part in repentance is to persistently decide to turn, or return, to God.

Grieving Our Losses

God sees your pain, your losses and your shame. He not only gives you permission to grieve your losses, but also He invites you to grieve. Grief is the process God created to help us deal with the inevitable losses of life. As you come to grips with the things that abortion has taken away from you, you can leave it at Jesus' feet—"where grace and mercy meet." God longs to comfort you and set you free so that you can lift your head.

While it may be painful, it is important to acknowledge the losses—those things, opportunities, people, relationships, experiences or feelings that abortion either has taken away from you or never allowed you to experience. If you like to journal, or you have followed my suggestion to keep a journal while you read this book, I strongly encourage you to write about the things God brings to your mind.

Close your eyes now and imagine Jesus walking into the room, putting His arms around you and gently speaking these words to you:

> Do not be afraid, for I have ransomed you. I have called you by name; you are mine. When you go through deep waters, I will be with you. When you go through rivers of difficulty, you will not drown. When you walk through the fire of oppression, you will not be burned up; the flames will not consume you. For I am the LORD, your God, the Holy One of Israel, your Savior (Isaiah 43:1-3, NLT).

At this point in your journey, it's important to understand what Jesus made possible at the cross. True and lasting freedom only comes as we understand the ransom price Jesus paid for our freedom and we accept His payment as our only hope of salvation and real life. If you have questions about accepting Jesus' sacrifice and free gift of eternal salvation, please ask your pastor, a Christian friend or another committed Christian to talk with you.

Steps to the Cross

- God created you and loves you (see Genesis 1:26-27; John 3:16-18).
- You (and everyone else) have fallen short of mankind's original glory at creation (see Genesis 3:1,13; Romans 3:23).
- Jesus came to rescue you from darkness and captivity (see Colossians 1:12-14).
- Jesus is your only hope for abundant and eternal life (see John 14:6).
- You must choose life (see John 1:12-13; John 5:24).

All Things Made New

Too often, we see ourselves as the sum of all our failures. We get blinded to who we really are and how God sees us after we've placed our trust in Jesus to rescue and redeem us. According to 2 Corinthians 5:17-18, if anyone is in Christ, he or she becomes a "new creation." This means that when you accept Christ as your Lord and Savior, you become new. Your old desires, your old inclinations and your old nature have been replaced with godly desires and a nature that He has given you. According to the verses from Ezekiel, God has given us His Spirit, which causes us to want to follow His ways.

> Therefore, if anyone is in Christ, the new creation has come: the old has gone, the new is here! All this is from God, who reconciled us to himself through Christ and gave us the ministry of reconciliation (2 Corinthians 5:17-18, *NIV*).

The Old Testament prophet Ezekiel provides a beautiful picture of the new life Christ gives for us:

> Then I will sprinkle clean water on you, and you will be clean; I will cleanse you from all your filthiness and from all your idols. Moreover, I will give you a new heart and put a new spirit within you; and I will remove the heart of stone from your flesh and give you a heart of flesh. I will put my Spirit within you and cause you to walk in My statutes, and you will be careful to observe My ordinances. . . you will be My people, and I will be your God (Ezekiel 36:25-28, *NASB*).

Amazingly, God makes us entirely new creations when we place our faith in Jesus. Why do many of us never experience much of the new creation God intends for us? There are three main reasons:

1. The enemy continues to deceive us, telling us that God doesn't care and that we're nothing.
2. We continue to live out of the well-worn patterns and ruts in our lives and don't embrace our new heart and new life.
3. We block the work of the Holy Spirit by resisting Him or turning away from God, going our own way and seeking satisfaction apart from Him.

God has so much more for you and for me. He has placed us in a favored position in His family, and we can step up to occupy that status as a favored daughter.

Your Favored Position in God's Family

God's love is lavished on those who place their faith in Jesus. Because of nothing other than God's extreme love for us, we've been given a position that few of us have grasped, and even fewer have lived in. Our enemy clearly wants to keep this hidden, but Scripture clearly tells us that we "did not receive a spirit of slavery to fall back into fear, but you received the Spirit of adoption, by whom we cry out, 'Abba, Father!' The Spirit Himself testifies together with our spirit that we are God's children" (Romans 8:15-16).

When we become children of God, we receive some amazing privileges. We are God's sons or daughters. We have literally been adopted into His family, but we also become heirs, which means we have an inheritance.

We've already been granted the privilege of the firstborn, but our position as royalty won't be fully revealed until Jesus returns in His glory. "When Christ, who is our life, is revealed, then you also will be revealed with Him in glory" (Colossians 3:4, *NASB*). We participate spiritually in His death, resurrection and glorification now. We're daughters of the King of kings, coheirs with Christ!

God wants this favored status to affect the way we approach life, the enemy and enslavement to past sins and failures. Romans 8:15 plainly says that we have received a spirit of adoption and not of slavery or fear. That should give us some boldness, sisters!

Trading Our Sorrow for Joy

The Bible is full of prophecies and promises that God will fulfill now in part and to the fullest extent when Jesus comes to take us into His eternal kingdom. Jeremiah 31 gives us one of these exciting prophecies for Israel, which also applies to Christ-followers under the New Covenant. Look at the passage and think how it fits both now and later.

They will come home and sing songs of joy on the heights of Jerusalem. They will be radiant because of the LORD's good gifts—the abundant crops of grain, new wine, and olive oil, and the healthy flocks and herds. Their life will be like a watered garden, and all their sorrows will be gone. The young women will dance for joy, and the men—old and young—will join in the celebration. I will turn their mourning into joy. I will comfort them and exchange their sorrow for rejoicing. The priests will enjoy abundance, and my people will feast on my good gifts. I, the LORD, have spoken! (Jeremiah 31:12-14, *NLT*).

Although life will still have troubles, God has given us His comfort, which should cause us to rejoice greatly. Read verse 13 again: God will turn our mourning into joy and our sorrow into rejoicing. Yes, even our sorrow. Trust me; but more important, trust Him.

Heart to Heart from Pat

You and I have come so very far on our journey, haven't we? God has helped you to confront what is possibly the darkest secret of your life. He has led you to truth about abortion that was hard but critical to hear and difficult to learn, but the truth has equipped you in a whole new way.

You have faced some painful memories, confronted some long-hidden horrors and drawn forth emotions you never even knew existed. You have confronted unhealthy anger that has been hindering your relationships and literally blocking your relationship with God. You have had a chance to place blame for your abortion choice, for your bad care, for your unfair treatment, and for your abandonment. But then there comes that moment when all else is moved aside and there is nothing left but you and God and your precious son or daughter.

I know that you have experienced many levels of the ultimate loss of your child, a loss that as women who have chosen abortion, we know to be a result of our own hand. We have destroyed our innocent children—bone of our bone and flesh of our flesh. In her book *The Desires of a Woman's Heart,* Beverly LaHaye refers to the words of a popular Hollywood actress who positioned herself as a proponent of a woman's right to abortion. One of her very public speeches proclaimed that despite the fact that abortion is the killing of an innocent, defenseless life, and that it hurts women emotionally, physically and spiritually, "it is my body, it is my nine months." Indeed, it was our bodies, wasn't it, sisters? It was our nine months. We are at a place in our journey where we have nowhere to look but at ourselves as the ultimate one responsible for our aborted children.

The very good news, however, is that we do not stop here in our own grief and loss. We have learned more than that now; we have learned that our Lord has paid the price for our decision. His blood was shed to cover our shame. He has rescued us from the results of our own sin.

This is the time in your journey for an exchange to take place. The grief you feel over the loss of your child is right and good; but it does not have to be destructive and crippling. You have looked at the wonderful teaching that Paul left with us from 2 Corinthians 7:9-11, teaching us that our distress, our sorrow, is to be used to draw us closer to our Lord. You have learned so far in your journey how to replace lies or false beliefs for truth. It is time for you to allow your sorrow to drive you into the arms of your Savior and exchange your sin for His Holiness. You are about to move to new heights; no more weights to dump, no more brush to clear. Now is the time to get refreshed and renewed.

Last year, my sweet husband gave me a beautiful necklace as a gift for our anniversary. It has a diamond clasp and was such a precious and extravagant gift that I absolutely loved it; in our 30-plus years of marriage, it was one of my favorite of all gifts. Somehow, somewhere, one day, I discovered it was missing. I searched everywhere that I could think of but the necklace was nowhere to be found. I was devastated and heartbroken. Not only had he paid a sacrificial amount of money for it, but also I felt so sad to have lost such a heartfelt treasure.

Months passed, and I thought of that necklace so very often, feeling so ashamed of my carelessness. The following Christmas, my dear husband handed me a beautifully wrapped box. Tucked inside was a new necklace, just like the one I had lost. That dear man had gone out and bought a necklace identical to the first to replace my own carelessly lost one.

The Scripture we have studied in Isaiah 43:1-3 this past chapter has become one of my most favorite and most often claimed passages in God's Word. Every time I read its proclamation, I am recharged in the power of God's goodness and my position in His family.

Ladies, we are daughters of the King of kings. It is more than time for us to take our places, to let the women of the world know who our Father is and what He has to say about abortion. It is more than time for our voices to be the ones making change and establishing laws. It is time for us to take back what belongs to us! Time to speak God's Word and truth on behalf of our daughters and friends. It is past time for our voices to be heard.

Let this session wash over you with its passion, cool you with its promise and cleanse your deepest loss with its peace. It is a gift to you from your Abba Father, a priceless gift that can never be lost.

JOURNAL TIME

Take some time after reading this chapter to write about and, more important, remember the day of your salvation.

1. When/where did you *surrender your life* to Jesus Christ?

2. Reread Isaiah 43:1-3 and express your feelings to God about being "ransomed" and called by name.

3. Express in your journal what your heart is feeling about God's amazing grace and unconditional love for you and for those involved in the heartbreak of abortion.

4. Spend some time thanking and praising God for all He has shown you so far in this study, and begin to ask Him for *His* plan for your next step in the journey.

_____

_____

_____

_____

_____

7

The Peace of Release ⇐ ⇐ ⇐

I have always been an avid reader and writer. I've kept a daily prayer journal for more than 20 years, chronicling my healing journey and pouring out my emotions. I keep a stash of yellowing, spiral-bound notebooks under my bed. They contain my story—the story of a broken woman rescued by a mighty God. They're so personal—full of testimonies to God's grace, but also of selfishness and silliness and whining—that I don't know what I want to do with them when I finally go home to Him.

But it was with the beginnings of those books that I took my first look into God's Word. Apart from the ambiguities of the world, God's Word answered my questions clearly. I remember when God showed me Psalm 139:13-16 (*NLT*):

> You made all the delicate, inner parts of my body and knit me together in my mother's womb. Thank you for making me so wonderfully complex! Your workmanship is marvelous—how well I know it. You watched me as I was being formed in utter seclusion, as I was woven together in the dark of the womb.
>
> You saw me before I was born. Every day of my life was recorded in your book. Every moment was laid out before a single day had passed.

As I envisioned my aborted child, my heart dropped. My grief encompassed me. As I learned how God felt about my baby—about every baby—I experienced fresh pain. I cried. I collapsed to the bedroom floor and buried my head in my arms. I cried out, this time to God, in sorrow and in the solitude of my significant loss.

Tears welled up from the depths of my soul, and it felt as if they'd never stop.

It was then that the Lord gave me a vision of a little girl in a frilly pink dress. She was beautiful and had long blonde hair and short arms outstretched to me. She smiled and then said, "It's okay, Mommy. I am happy here with Jesus. I forgive you and love you. I'll be here waiting when you come, but Jesus has some things for you to do first."

Little did I know all that He had in mind for my complete healing and restoration.

He has the same dream to heal and restore you!

He has. . . *more than you can hope or imagine.*

More Than I Could Imagine

"Surreal" is the best word to describe my feelings as I walked down the long white hospital corridor leading into the Neonatal Intensive Care Unit (NICU) of Tampa's largest women's hospital. The space was filled with white walls, white ceilings and bare windows. An emotional battle raged in my heart and head. My husband and I walked the seemingly endless hallway together just as we had so many years before. This day, we were here to meet our soon-to-be baby daughter. Our hearts were drawn to meet her. But my head was stuck in memories of another time when we had taken a similar walk down a different corridor in this same hospital. Twelve years earlier, we'd had an abortion here. It all seemed so bizarre. The circumstances of each event were amazing in different ways.

As Mike and I rounded the corner of the NICU into the open nursery area, we were both trembling, gripping hands so tightly that it threatened to cut off all feeling in my hand. The room was filled with babies. Most were lying inside clear plastic boxes with two little "portholes" in the front for the doctors and nurses to slip their hands through when caring for the sick and tiny babies. Some babies lay naked with tiny arms and legs flailing wildly, and all kinds of tubes and wires attached to them for the monitoring of every body function. They lay on chest-high podium-like tables covered with soft, white sheepskin.

That is how we first saw her—such a tiny baby girl, *tiny* being the key word. The nurses had named her Julianna; Juli for July, the month of her birth, and Anna for the prophetic beauty of the name.

Julianna had been born to a 17-year-old girl at approximately 23 weeks' gestation. Her birth weight was a whopping 1-1/2 pounds! She was 10 inches long. The day we met Julianna, she had recently undergone some surgery and her weight had dropped to only one pound. She was barely the size of a matchbox!

Without question, she was one of the most incredible and beautiful things I had ever seen. As I looked upon her face for the first time, doctors and nurses gathered around to see for themselves the couple that had come to adopt Julianna. They were very protective and concerned. I felt like I was in a trance. It took all I had to stay upright and not swoon to the floor as I heard the sweet voice of God speak to my heart, "This, Pat, is what I create in a mother's womb; this is why I have called you to do the work I have called you to do." I felt overwhelming surety that God had literally placed a "pre-born" child in my presence.

As I looked upon Julianna, my mind was reeling from that very reality: "the work" He had recently "called me to do." I was very certain that God had called me not many months before to open Tampa, Florida's first crisis pregnancy center. As I stood beside that tiny baby lying in the center of that white, sheepskin-covered table, a large group of my closest friends were hard at work back at my insurance agency painting, wallpapering and preparing some vacant space in the back half of my office in order for that to become a reality. I had "recruited" them to join the vision God had given me, and they had eagerly responded.

We were set to open in just a few more months. God was clearly leading the way, and His favor preceded our every move. I was running my own insurance business out of the front office and preparing for ministry out of the back. Donations of paint, wallpaper, office supplies, pregnancy tests and furniture were coming from every direction. And on and on the blessings flowed.

From the moment I had asked Christ into my heart, He moved into my life in a mighty way. He surrounded me with strong Christian mentors who were committed to helping me learn as much as I could about God and His ways. They taught me to love the Word of God and to pray. They were relentless in their unconditional love as the many walls of my past and my pain had to crumble to set me on a whole new path. The Lord knew how important these friends would be to me as I struggled to believe that He could truly forgive a past as sinful as mine.

I will never forget the day He gently revealed the truth about abortion to me. My immediate temptation was to hide away and never tell my Christian friends. I was convinced that once they knew the horrible truth, they could not accept me anymore. Of course, I was very wrong. Not only did they accept and love me, but they also became the wind under my wings as they encouraged me into the plans God had for my life. What an awesome God He is, thinking through every detail!

As I stood amidst the flurry of activity within the NICU, my thoughts swirled over the events of the past few days . . .

My life was a daily nonstop wave of activity as I ran a full-time insurance agency and parented two sons, an 18-year-old senior in high school and a preteen 10-year-old. All the while, I was deeply involved in the excitement of preparing to open a crisis pregnancy center. It was in the midst of all this when my husband, Mike, woke up one morning and announced, "I think we should adopt a baby girl!" My response wasn't exactly overflowing with Proverbs 31 qualities when I responded in my old Pat ways with, "Are you crazy?! Can't you see how busy my life is? Does it look like I have time for a baby? Besides, we have a senior!" Needless to say, I was shocked and a bit miffed.

Mike and I had discussed the possibility of adoption on several occasions. We had two sons, and I had longed for a daughter for many years. I had always believed in my heart that my aborted child was a little girl. Adoption had just never happened; it was too expensive and too much red tape. How to start? Time passed, and it was only small talk until that day I told Mike it was impossible. It was bad timing. No way! Fortunately with God, *nothing* is impossible. His ways are not our ways!

Mike arrived home from work that same afternoon looking frazzled and pale. He had taken the liberty, as only a man would do, of inquiring of an attorney friend of ours that day at work about the possibilities of adopting a child, maybe a toddler. "Do you believe in divine intervention?" the friend asked Mike. "Absolutely. . . why?" Mike replied.

Our friend proceeded to tell Mike that He had just hung up the phone with the hospital and they had a baby girl the birth mother desired to place for adoption. Our friend knew that the 60-something families he had on his list would probably be skeptical about this adoption. He told Mike, "This little girl was born three months early and weighs only one pound. She is likely to have serious life-long health challenges. She will possibly be blind, unable to hear and could be retarded. It is difficult to determine and probably will be for a long time. We are not even certain she will live." Mike relayed our morning conversation to our friend, promptly assuring him that I would probably not be interested but he would talk to me that night.

We sat on our bedside while my husband relayed the remarkable story to me that evening. We were both overwhelmed with emotion. In typical "Pat" fashion, I got right to work. I decided to call everyone I knew who was interested in adopting a child. The first person I called was one of my very dear "God friends," Elaine. Elaine and I had become friends through a ministry we had founded together called Sisters of Rachel, a healing ministry for women who have had abortions.

Elaine had an abortion during her late teens. That aborted child turned out to be the only child she would ever be able to conceive. She was unable to become pregnant again and longed for a child. She listened intently to Julianna's story. Then she was very quiet on the other end of the telephone.

"What do you think, Elaine?" I asked her.

"I think I would absolutely love to have that little girl, but I can't," she replied.

"Why not, Elaine? God will work all this out. He can bring this child through. I know He can."

"Oh, I am certain that He will bring her through," Elaine said, "but this baby is not for me. . . God planned this little girl for you and Mike!"

I can remember the chair I was sitting in, the level of the sun outside the window, the clarity of the blue sky and the tears that rolled down my cheeks. That little tiny girl I have never seen is going to be my daughter. Mike's and mine. Julianna *is* for us. I called Mike at work and we agreed to meet at the hospital to see our daughter for the first time.

It was love at first sight for both of us. We knew immediately and without a single moment's doubt that God had delivered Julianna to us. Mike and I spent the next three months going back and forth to the hospital. Sometimes twice in one day. Each time I went to see Julianna, I would lay my hands upon her in her isolate and pray Psalm 139 and Jeremiah 1 over her. "Julianna, God knit you together in your mother's womb; you are fearfully and wonderfully made. God knows the plans He has for you, Julianna. They are plans for good and not for evil, you will live and not die."

Mike and I and all of our friends and family stood in faith for complete and perfect health for our baby girl. It was not an effortless or faultless faith. Sometimes, I would cry all the way home from the hospital and ask Mike, "What if she doesn't make it?" He would gently remind me of how God had pulled this together and that He had planned for us to be her mommy and daddy. She needed us.

Sometimes our friends and family would weaken, not so sure about just what we were getting ourselves into. We became very close to Julianna's doctors and her main nurse, Jayne. As we did, we learned more and more of the miracle details of her birth and rescue from death. Not a single NICU team member could deny the miracle of her life or her undefeatable spirit. Mike and I were always aware of what an honor and a privilege we had been given.

Julianna came home with us three months later. She had a head full of blonde hair, perfectly shaped tiny rosy lips and beautiful pink skin. She was a perfectly healthy four pounds. No complications. No health problems. Nothing missing or broken.

Today, Julianna is a beautiful young woman who loves God and loves life.

How precious and great is our God!

So far, you have:

- Boldly stepped beyond fear and came forward to trust God with your secret pain;

- Shared your secret;

- Learned the truth about abortion and faced some difficult facts about the life of precious children lost to abortion;

- Faced anger and unforgiveness of others involved in abortion;

- Looked into the face of your Lord to understand your own sin and receive His marvelous mercy, grace and forgiveness. You must choose life (see John 1:12-13; John 5:24).

Now is the time for you to acknowledge and grieve the life of the precious child you lost to abortion. It may seem odd to acknowledge your baby's life, but it is really completely natural.

A dear friend of mine lost her firstborn child at birth. When the doctor placed her stillborn baby girl in her arms to hold and tell her good-bye, he uttered some very wise words: "Before you can mourn her death, you must acknowledge her life."

In this step of your healing journey, you are going to do what your heart has desired to do for a long time. God has led you to this place. He has held you and comforted you through each step of this very difficult journey. He has embraced you in His arms as you have come to terms with your anger and your grief. He is with you now and is leading you as you acknowledge your grief and say good-bye to the child you lost.

You are at a crucial and special place in your healing journey. This is the place where you can see your wounds healed, your broken heart mended and find reconciliation with your child. Here, you exchange bondage for freedom, fear for courage and shame for enduring joy.

While this is a time of closure, it is also a time of new beginnings. We can choose life. You can begin living in the light of God's redemptive healing.

Remember that you are God's child and are deeply loved by your Father. As you continue to face the loss of your child, you have permission to mourn, to accept comfort and to comfort others who know the same pain you have suffered.

Heart to Heart from Pat

Wow! The majesty of God is overwhelming. The victory found in your journey with God is well worth the process, isn't it? You and I have made it to the top. I promised you at the beginning of this journey that we would get here and that you would be a different woman.

Was I right? My guess is that God has done the most amazing things in your life over these past several weeks. That is not to say that all of the work God is doing in your life is done. Oh no! God's work in you—in all of us—is a process. God will continue to heal your heart and show you more that He has for you.

For several years after that first book encounter, God continued to work out many things in my life. He continued to work out the issues and attitudes that led to my abortion as well as the things that followed—the bad decisions and choices. Each woman who shared her story with me brought out new things hidden in my heart that I had shoved aside or refused to admit.

Regardless of the timing or the individual process God uses, I have never taken any woman on this journey in more than 20 years that I have not watched God change before my very eyes. It has been the most amazing privilege—one that I will be challenging you to accept in the next chapter. We'll talk about that more later. But for now, even though I cannot see you, I am certain that your face is different than it was when you stepped into this dreaded mountain climb. You have accomplished so much.

Do you remember the story of Esther in the Bible? I love that story. In fact, I have loved it so much over the years that I have transferred that love to my own daughter who now claims it as her favorite. The thing I love most about Esther is her courage. She never signed up for her assignment; putting her pretty little neck on the line was not her idea of a good time. But God had a plan, and she, in her obedience and love for God, followed His plan to the salvation of a nation.

God also has a plan for you. He chose you for this journey. He wants you healed and whole and ready to be given an assignment that will change the world, just like He did with Esther. But first, you have to end at the beginning. Remember how, at the start of our journey, we had to understand how going back is sometimes required for moving forward? We are kind of at that place again.

This chapter ends with a bittersweet assignment. You are asked to write a letter, a poem or a song to your unborn child or children. I know that your heart is full of loss and sorrow over the child of your heart who is missing from your life. I know, because I have a daughter who is standing with yours. God, in His tender mercy, allowed me to see her in that special way that we see things from God. She was whole and joyful. She was full of grace and mercy for me.

I actually saw her reach out to me and comfort *me*. Imagine that! (I believe that you probably can.) She assured me of her place with the Lord and her anticipation of the day when we would be together in heaven, the day that she would meet both of her brothers and her own precious sister.

You must know that you will never completely walk away from the longing to embrace your lost child; but also know that God's grace is sufficient for you. He will give you an everlasting peace that when you think of your son or daughter, His peace is bigger than your grief and loss. Let God complete the work He has begun in you, in His time. Trust Him, and do not waver. Just trust!

Surrender your life to Him and He will take you on a new journey that you would not believe even if you were told!

Look at the nations and watch—and be utterly amazed. For I am going to do something in your days that you would not believe, even if you were told (Habakkuk 1:5, *NIV*).

JOURNAL TIME

Take some time to write a letter to your unborn child or to the other children you are acknowledging. It may be to your grandchild or your niece or nephew. Write the child a letter expressing God's great love for all of life created by Him and for Him. You may want to go to a sweet, quiet place and write the letter, telling of your sorrow and your love. Choose a flower or a memorial marker to leave in that place as you release your child to the loving hands of God. If you have surrendered your heart to Christ, you can rest assured that you will see him or her again. You will hold your son or daughter in your arms and you will get back what the enemy intended to steal.

If there is someone you know who would understand this journey, make arrangements to share your letter with that person. If you haven't done so before, *now* is the time to contact us at the Surrendering the Secret national office for help. In the meantime, let me pray for you.

Lord, I thank You for Your grace. I thank You that You work all things together for good for those who love You, according to Your purpose. I thank You for the deeper personal relationship that I now have with You. In my weakness, I have found Your strength. I pray that You will place the desire in my heart to share this journey with other women and reach out to them as You have reached out to me, sharing the freedom and joy that You have secured for us.

Before you move on, take some time to read and write out God's plan for your future as you consider these truths.

Trust in the Lord with all your heart, and do not rely on your own understanding; think about Him in all your ways, and He will guide you on the right paths (Proverbs 3:5-6).

"For I know the plans I have for you," declares the Lord, "plans to prosper you and not to harm you, plans to give you hope and a future. Then you will call upon me and come and pray to me, and I will listen to you. You will seek me and find me when you seek me with all your heart" (Jeremiah 29:11-13, *NIV*).

Read what Jesus has done with your past failures and sins:

Surely our griefs He Himself bore, and our sorrows He carried; yet we ourselves esteemed Him stricken, smitten of God, and afflicted. But He was pierced through for our transgressions, He was crushed for our iniquities; the chastening for our well-being fell upon Him, and by His scourging we are healed (Isaiah 53:4-5, *NASB*).

Let all that I am praise the LORD; may I never forget the good things he does for me. He forgives all my sins and heals all my diseases. He redeems me from death and crowns me with love and tender mercies. . . . For his unfailing love toward those who fear him is as great as the height of the heavens above the earth. He has removed our sins from us as far as the east is from the west. The LORD is like a father to his children, tender and compassionate to those who fear him (Psalm 103:2-4,11-13, *NLT*).

Life. . .

- Not only is your child fully human from the moment of conception, but also he or she has already been given a personal, eternal soul.

- All prenatal existence is linked to a postnatal life. The life of your soul is an eternal spiritual continuum that begins at conception and continues into eternity.

- God placed inestimable value on your child from the moment of conception; he or she was created and deeply loved by God.

At death, the unborn child immediately passes into the presence of God. Each little one is present with the Father. They have identity and individuality; they deserve to be known for who they are: eternal beings. They still have a divine purpose that, though it may transcend our understanding for the moment, we shall perceive clearly when the day dawns that we no longer see through a glass darkly but face-to-face.

Read the story of David and Bathsheba found in 2 Samuel 11 and 12. David's sin led to the loss of his son. He, like us, was the reason the child did not survive. Yet he was also called "a man after God's own heart," a man who understood his own failure and repented of it. David's God is our God; his promises are our promises. Listen to what the Bible says about seeing your child again someday:

[King] David replied, "I fasted and wept while the child was alive, for I said, 'Perhaps the LORD will be gracious to me and let the child live.' But why should I fast when he is dead? Can I bring him back again? I will go to him one day, but he cannot return to me" (2 Samuel 12:22-23, *NLT*).

Do not be afraid, for I am with you; I will bring your children from the east and gather you from the west. I will say to the north, "Give them up!" and to the south, "Do not hold them back." Bring my sons from afar and my daughters from the ends of the earth—everyone who is called by my name, whom I created for my glory, whom I formed and made (Isaiah 43:5-7, *NIV*).

Passing It On!

I had stepped from my house into my garage with a giant bag of hand-me-down clothes to share with my younger sister. And as I stepped through the door, I was caught by the sound of men's voices strained by emotion. I quickly discovered my husband and our middle child, sitting in the middle of our garage, huddled in a heap of tears. It took me a minute to register in my head what I was seeing. They were supposed to be mowing the lawn for goodness' sake. What in the world had happened?

I soon discovered that the two of them had somehow landed in a discussion about the abortion my husband and I had so many years before. My husband was set to join me in sharing our testimony at an upcoming event for our local pregnancy center ministry. We had always shared openly with our children about these past choices. All three of them had been raised with the open sharing, speaking and writing that God had called me into.

At the time of this encounter, our son was about 17 and had apparently asked my husband some clarifying questions about what all had happened. As my son listened to his dad reflect upon his heartbreak, he began for the first time to embrace his own personal loss of a baby sister. You might imagine what came down on our garage floor that day as the three of us wept and grieved afresh the loss of an innocent part of our family.

On that day, two things happened that changed me forever. One, God healed my heart just a little bit more; and two, I made a fresh commitment to Him to share with anyone, anytime He asked me to, so that the next generation, my son and his children would not buy the same lie his dad and I had fallen for.

I am committed to challenging and encouraging women and men who have had abortions to seek healing; to understand God's redeeming love; then to openly share the truth so that their children and grandchildren will be spared this holocaust.

Just like the bag of hand-me-down clothes that were headed to my sister that one life-changing morning in the garage, we can, and do, pass on what we have not cleaned up! Let's clean this up for those coming after us. Let's tell them the truth. The word of *our* testimony is *their* only hope.

You and I have traveled an amazing journey together. We are not the same people who came together when you first picked up this book. We are not the same women who were afraid of what we might find in its pages and feared to face the truth and pain of the dark secret of abortion. God has been good. He has begun a powerful work of healing in you, and He has brought you to a new time and place. Even though the path ahead is unfamiliar, you are ready to move forward into all He has in store for you.

Your Ongoing Journey

As we close our journey together, please realize that completing a book full of steps doesn't mean your journey is complete. It's actually just the beginning. This time with me has been only one chapter in your story.

> All the days ordained for me were written in your book before one of them came to be (Psalm 139:16, *NIV*).

> You've kept track of my every toss and turn through the sleepless nights, each tear entered in your ledger, each ache written in your book... I'm proud to praise God, proud to praise GOD. Fearless now, I trust in God; what can mere mortals do to me? God, you did everything you promised, and I'm thanking you with all my heart. You pulled me from the brink of death, my feet from the cliff-edge of doom. Now I stroll at leisure with God in the sunlit fields of life (Psalm 56:8,10-13, *THE MESSAGE*).

God is calling you into a great adventure. He has a unique role just for you. As you step outside yourself to engage in the larger story, acknowledge that completing the first pass through the eight steps doesn't mean there's nothing for you. Here is some of what God has in store for you as you continue your journey with Him:

> I [God] will restore to you the years that the swarming locust has eaten, the crawling locust, the consuming locust, and the chewing locust (Joel 2:25, *NKJV*).

Locusts are ravenous creatures, devouring life as they swarm. In this passage, locusts represent the torment or consequences that have come into our lives as a result of bad decisions that we or other people have made. In our case, they clearly represent the pain of abortion that has chewed up our lives and relationships.

> I pray that out of his glorious riches he may strengthen you with power through his Spirit in your inner being, so that Christ may dwell in your hearts through faith. And I pray that you, being rooted and established in love, may have power, together with all the Lord's holy people, to grasp how wide and long and high and deep is the love of Christ, and to know this love that surpasses knowledge—that you may be filled to the measure of all the fullness of God. Now to him who is able to do immeasurably more than all we ask or imagine, according to his power that is at work within us, to him be glory in the church and in Christ Jesus throughout all generations, for ever and ever! Amen (Ephesians 3:16-21, *NIV*).

> We declare God's wisdom, a mystery that has been hidden and that God destined for our glory before time began. . . . As it is written: "What no eye has seen, what no ear has heard, and what no human mind has conceived"—the things God has prepared for those who love him (1 Corinthians 2:7,9, *NIV*).

The Power of Your Story

God's provision for the past is more than sufficient, and His promises for the future are incredibly bright! God invites us to become instruments of His love, His life and His healing power. He has led us on a path of healing; now He wants to use our stories to help others. Our goal now must be to discover and pursue Gold's purposes for our lives.

Revelation 12:11 shows the power of our stories as it talks about the larger story and the coming final battle between good and evil:

> They triumphed over him [Satan] by the blood of the Lamb [Jesus] and by the word of their testimony; they did not love their lives so much as to shrink from death (Revelation 12:11, *NIV*).

In Revelation 12:11, "they" refers to us—Jesus' followers. "Him" who will be overcome refers to the enemy. Three things are crucial in overcoming the work of the enemy. How can each of our stories or testimonies be powerful in the battle?

Live Your Story

Remember three key truths as you pursue your role in God's larger story:

Key 1: God wants us to live for something greater than ourselves!

> For everything, absolutely everything, above and below, visible and invisible, rank after rank after rank of angels—*everything* got started in him and finds its purpose in him (Colossians 1:16, *THE MESSAGE*).

> I chose you before I formed you in the womb; I set you apart before you were born. I appointed you a prophet to the nations (Jeremiah 1:5).

Key 2: We are saved to serve God! We are healed to serve others!

> Don't be ashamed of the testimony about our Lord, or of me His prisoner. Instead, share in suffering for the gospel, relying on the power of God. He has saved us and called us with a holy calling, not according to our works, but according to His own purpose and grace, which was given to us in Christ Jesus before time began (2 Timothy 1:8-9).

Don't you know that your body is a sanctuary of the Holy
Spirit who is in you, whom you have from God? You are not
your own, for you were bought at a price. Therefore glorify
God in your body (1 Corinthians 6:19-20).

Key 3: God's power is revealed in our weakness.

Brothers, consider your calling: not many are wise from a
human perspective, not many powerful, not many of noble
birth. Instead, God has chosen what is foolish in the world
to shame the wise, and God has chosen what is weak in
the world to shame the strong. God has chosen what is
insignificant and despised in the world—what is viewed as
nothing—to bring to nothing what is viewed as something,
so that no one can boast in His presence. But it is from Him
that you are in Christ Jesus, who became God-given wisdom
for us—our righteousness, sanctification, and redemption
(1 Corinthians 1:26-30).

According to this passage, what kind of people does God choose
to use for His rescue mission in our world? What turns people like
us into heroes (see verse 30)?

Set Hearts Free

As we learn to accept and appreciate who we are in Christ, and who
He is in us, God has an adventure waiting for us. Read Isaiah 61:1-3
aloud, replacing the word "me" with your name.

The Spirit of the Sovereign LORD is on me, because the
LORD has anointed me to preach good news to the poor.
He has sent me to bind up the brokenhearted, to proclaim
freedom for the captives and release from darkness for the
prisoners, to proclaim the year of the LORD'S favor and the
day of vengeance of our God, to comfort al who mourn, and
provide for those who grieve in Zion—to bestow on them
a crown of beauty instead of ashes, the oil of joy instead of
mourning, and a garment of praise instead of a spirit of
despair (Isaiah 61:1-3, *NIV*).

As you join with Jesus in His mission to bind up the broken-hearted, to set captives free and to replace beauty for ashes, you won't believe how exciting and deeply fulfilling it can be!

Praise the God and Father of our Lord Jesus Christ, the Father of mercies and the God of all comfort. He comforts us in all our affliction, so that we may be able to comfort those who are in any kind of affliction; through the comfort we ourselves receive from God. For as the sufferings of Christ overflow to us, so through Christ our comfort also overflows (2 Corinthians 1:3-5).

But thanks be to God, who always leads us in triumph in Christ, and manifests through us the sweet aroma of the knowledge of Him in every place. For we are a fragrance of Christ to God among those who are being saved and among those who are perishing; to the one an aroma from death to death, to the other an aroma from life to life. And who is adequate for these things? (2 Corinthians 2:14-16, *NASB*).

Some Thoughts to Ponder

- How is God the Father portrayed in 2 Corinthians 1:3 and 2:14? How does this portrayal compare to your deepest heart's beliefs about God?

- How do you think your past wounds and brokenness enhance your usefulness to God and His work of comforting, healing and setting captives free (see 2 Corinthians 1:4-5)?

- What world-changing challenge is placed in our hands in 2 Corinthians 2:15-16? How would you answer Paul's question "Who is adequate for these things?"

Look again at these two passages from the perspective of what you receive, rather than from the perspective of what you give. What are the benefits to your own recovery and healing as you share with others and become God's "triumph" and a "sweet aroma" (2 Corinthians 1:4-5; 2:15-16)?

The amazing thing is that as you work with Jesus in setting captives free, you'll find that one captive who becomes more increasingly liberated is you! God has made some amazing promises to you if you are willing to raise your eyes to Him (above your current pain) and embrace the larger story. These promises give powerful incentive not to give up but to continue on to still more.

Thousands of women and men, bound by secret abortions, are sitting in our churches and are living as our neighborhoods; they may even be our closest friends. Your sharing of your past could help set them free. As Revelation 12:11 illustrates, unmatchable power lies in your willingness to be vulnerable.

Using wisdom and prayer to guide your sharing is very important. God would not have you injure or hurt others in the process of sharing. He will show you how, when, where and with whom to share.

Heart to Heart from Pat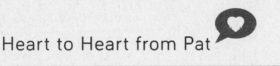

I have to tell you that, as we close this time we have spent together, my sincere and heartfelt prayer is that we will someday meet face-to-face.

I have been married to the same man for more than 36 years. We have three children, five grandchildren and two beautiful daughters by marriage to our sons. We have family in heaven, including our daughter lost to abortion and a grandson lost just before his birth. We have a marriage that has survived purely by God's grace.

God has used us, despite the ugliness of our past, the bad choices and the constant failures, to make a difference in the lives of others—prayerfully, in your life!

I am a woman who is living her story. God wants the same thing from each one of us. He wants to use your story in the lives of others!

Revelation 12:11 says that we overcome the work of the enemy in three ways:

1. *The precious atoning blood of Jesus.* Nothing surpasses that. He alone is our Savior, our Redeemer, our merciful Lord. He is our one and only, our all in all!

2. *By the word of our testimony.* Second only to Jesus' atoning blood is our testimony. God uses our stories to establish His kingdom here on earth. Imagine that, my friend! Not only does our Lord rescue us and remove our sin, but He also wants us to be part of His salvation message to the world. It is more than my little brain can understand, but it is true. I have lived it, and I have seen it. The fact that you are reading my book today is no less than a miracle at the level of parting the Red Sea and raising people from the dead. Never in my wildest hopes or dreams would this be happening. Not only because of my past sin but also because of my ever-present and daily failures! God continues to show me that His Word means business. He wants to use broken but surrendered women. I believe that you are one of those women.

3. *"They did not love their lives so much as to shrink from death."* I am not a Bible scholar, but I have read many studies of Revelation 12. The book in its entirety fascinates me because John uses the analogy of a woman and her child in the final battle against the enemy. Someday, I will take the time to pursue God's interpretation of those words for women today; but for now, I have come to understand that last part of Revelation 12:11 to mean that I must be willing to *surrender* the life that I might think I want for myself. I have to be willing to symbolically "die" to some of the things I want for my life, some of the things that other people think I should do with my life. I have to let that all go for the number one thing God has called me to do: live my story through the word of my testimony—spoken, written and shared one on one.

The fact that abortion is the law of the land, that most churches have no voice against it, and that women and men are hidden in their own shame and secrets is surely a heartbreak to God.

We must tell someone.

We must reach out to our silent sisters and brothers and draw them out.

We must be willing to tell our stories so that others can be healed and set free. I have watched what God has done with women who are set free just by my own transparency, by hearing my own story. Free men and women change the world.

I encourage you to prayerfully consider what God would have you do with this healing in your life. Consider starting a *Surrendering the Secret* Bible study in your church or sharing your testimony at a ladies' retreat, writing it out for your church newsletter or taking your story to your local crisis pregnancy center for them to use with other women. Talk to your pastor, your women's ministry leader or your church's counseling pastor. Tell someone what God has done in your life. *Do not* let the enemy hold your secret any longer.

As we part, I hope to hear from you. I want to hear how your journey has progressed and what God is doing with your ministry of restoration.

Let me close our work together with the words that ring most loudly in my heart with this ministry and with what I truly see God doing through this process in all of our lives:

> Now to Him who, by the power that is at work within us, is able to carry out His purposes and do superabundantly, far over and above all that we dare ask or think—infinitely beyond our highest prayers, desires, thoughts, hopes, or dreams—To Him be glory in the church and in Christ Jesus throughout all generations forever and ever. Amen (Ephesians 3:20-21, *AMP*).

JOURNAL TIME

1. What cautions might you need to exercise as you begin to share your story with others? Consider your motives. Be sensitive with others, and ask God how to wait for His leading in sharing your abortion experience before you step out publicly.

_____

_____

_____

_____

_____

2. With whom might you speak privately before sharing your abortion publicly? Your husband? Your parents? Your children? By being brave, and trusting God, you may save someone from making the same choice.

_____

_____

_____

_____

3. Brainstorm with someone you trust some ways that you can use your healing from abortion to reach out to other women who are hurting and still in bondage.

_____

_____

_____

_____

Establish some sort of accountability about how you will serve God in helping others as you have been helped. The statistics from chapter 3 indicated that 43 percent of women of childbearing age have been broken by abortion. Only the truth, which you now have, can help set them free.

4. How willing are you to participate in the adventure of setting hearts free? What, if any, reservations do you have?

_____

_____

_____

_____

5. What unique gifts, talents, resources and life experiences has God given you to comfort hurting people, to release them from bondage or to show them the way to Jesus so that they can find redemption from shame and failure?

_____

_____

_____

_____

6. How might people respond to your encouragement that there is a way out of their problems, pain and destructive behaviors?

_____

_____

_____

_____

Continually review chapter 6 to remind yourself of God's promise to you. Keep God's Word in your mouth and in your heart. Remember, we have decided to choose life!

Epilogue

Think back to the first time you opened this book. You will remember that the common thread you share with thousands of women and men is the experience of an abortion. It is that painful experience that connects you. Thousands more could identify with you as a result of that experience. They need you, and they need your story.

Now that you have completed your journey, you can identify with others in a new way. You are *set free* by God's forgiveness, hope and grace. You are a woman of strength and courage who has climbed a mountain to the top.

Your identity is no longer that of a post-abortive woman or man. You are a child of God, of truth and integrity, and your identity is in Christ and who He says you are. You are a new creation in Christ. What once appeared to be an unscalable mountain when viewed from below is now under your feet. God has been faithful to do what He said He would do. He has set the captives free. He has set *you* free!

Although you've completed *A Surrendered Life,* the rest of your life is a continuing journey with Christ. There will always be mountains to climb until you reach your heavenly destination. So as you go forward, be good to yourself, take time to love yourself, smile inwardly and keep your sense of humor.

My love and blessings,
Pat

Sharing the Secret with Your Children

During the past many years of watching women walk the journey of healing through a *Surrendering the Secret* Bible study, the most common roadblock to using a past abortion as a Revelation 12:11 opportunity—the word of our testimony—is the fear of telling our children.

Let me assure you, my friend, you must tell.

You must be willing, in God's timing, to tell your precious sons and daughters that you are a sinner saved by grace.

You may discover a whole new level of love come from your transparency and surrender to God's leading.

If we want to save our children from the same mistakes, we must tell.

I wrote a recent article about my own challenges with this very topic. Following my article are two other stories from women who are using the word of their testimony to help others.

"What is this book, G," my oldest granddaughter asked from her seat behind me in the car.

My heart dropped. I'd forgotten that I'd left some of my *Surrendering the Secret* books in a basket on the floorboard of my car. As a brand-new reader, she grabbed everything with writing on it to test her newfound skill.

"It has your name on it. Did you write this, G?"

"Yes, I did; it's a Bible study."

"Can we read it?"

"Yes, someday I'll read it to you, beautiful girl."

Oh my. Someday, I will have to talk to my precious, adorable granddaughter about my abortion. Someday, I will have to tell her about my sin, my loss and my restoration through Jesus. Someday; but not today.

She is only eight years old.

It has been over 40 years since abortion-on-demand became the law of the land in the United States after the Supreme Court ruled 5-4 in favor of the plaintiff in *Roe v. Wade*. In those 40+ years, 55 million unborn American babies have become fatalities of abortion.

The Bible places particular significance on the number 40. The pages of Scripture are filled with events and people whose stories are marked off by that number, which represents a generation.

Consider Moses and the Israelites, who wandered 40 years in the wilderness just outside of the Promised Land, until the old, rebellious generation was gone and a new generation arose to take its place.

What a humbling concept as we consider the shedding of innocent blood—which God hates (see Proverbs 6:17)—that has been legally endorsed for the past 40+ years. America has lost nothing less than a generation.

For my part, I am missing a daughter, along with nieces and nephews, precious children of friends, and friends I'll never know because they were never allowed to take a breath on this earth.

Little did I know the devastation and loss of innocent life that would be the result of my articles, petitions and politics. Little did I know that my own ignorance and selfishness would lead me to opt for abortion.

Little did I know that my own precious unborn daughter would be one of those lost lives. Little did I know that someday, I would have to share that story with my own granddaughter.

As we have passed this life-changing fortieth anniversary of *Roe v. Wade* on January 22, 2013, I am still passionate, vocal and pro-choice. However, this time, my pro-choice message declares the words of Deuteronomy 30:19:

I have set before you life and death—choose life so
that you and your children may live.

I am now counting on a new promise, found in Revelation 12:11, which assures me that we Christians conquer even our worst enemies—even Satan himself—by "the blood of the Lamb and by the word of [our] testimony."

It has become my life's passion and calling to do all I can to protect and defend the next generation. I am thankful to have been able to share my story in *A Surrendered Life*.

Maybe I will read it to my granddaughter. Someday.

Another Mother/Daughter Story
of the Power of Forgiveness

Mom's Story—Going Back to Go Forward

The most difficult journey is to go back to the place where you failed. So difficult, that I had managed to avoid that journey for more than 25 years! Suddenly, I was there; the journey was quick to an unexpected, unplanned (by me) *moment of truth* . . .

Jenni, my young-adult daughter, and I had met at a Starbucks to plan a girl's weekend for the senior high students I was teaching at my church. We were going to study a book with them titled *When God Writes Your Love Story*. In the middle of our planning (in the middle of Starbucks!), Jenni put down her pen, faced me with a look that portrayed surprise, confidence and even expectancy, and said, "Mom, I can't seem to shake an overwhelming sense that there's something you need to tell me."

Well, my heart started racing in about a million different directions, but my mind was stayed on what I knew God was doing. You see, I had prayed for this moment, a chance to tell Jenni, but now? *Not now!* In my mind, I wrestled with God for what seemed liked hours before I managed to open my mouth and speak.

Body trembling and tears falling, I began sharing my secret story. "Well, honey, you remember that I told you a few years ago, because you asked, that your dad and I had indeed had sex *before* we were married? Well, I have managed to skirt around the rest of the story—until now. The rest of the story being that I got pregnant, and—well, there is no baby, so you can probably guess what happened."

Her reply? "No, Mom, I can't guess; I have no idea what happened." God was going to make *me* say the "word," sure enough! Eyes downcast with shame, and giant tears falling by now, I spoke the truth: "At age 18, I had an abortion."

Expecting horror in her eyes, I saw love. Waiting for the words "Mom, how could you?" I heard instead, "Mom, I'm so sorry you went through that." And then she said, "*Mom, this just explains so much!*"

Truth brings understanding. Suddenly, pieces of life made sense to her—things like my nervous reactions to her teenage years, especially her dating years; my and her dad's marriage problems; our near-divorce, our fights, and so much more. And when I heard her words, I realized that abortion had affected every part of my life.

I also knew, without a doubt, that it was God who had prompted her question, and it was He who had brought me on the journey to this moment, to this *surrendering of my secret.*

The very next week, Jenni sent me a beautiful card in which she wrote, "Mom, for as long as I have been alive, you have given yourself and more for me. The one thing I could not ask of you, because I did not know to ask of you, was for your *truth.*" That precious daughter, a gift from God, *thanked* me for sharing what I needed to release, what she needed to hear!

Telling the truth set me free!

Truth set *both* of us free—to love the Word of God together, to grow and share and speak truth to others!

"Let's tell them," she said. "Tell them we are *not* slaves to fear/guilt/sin. *We are free!*" Can I hear a hallelujah?

God started a journey that day, using my own precious daughter, to display the kind of love and freedom He had waiting for me. He drew the truth out of me. He journeyed me back to the place I had failed, not to shame me, but to free me from its grip on my past, my present and my future! And the journey continued, taking me places where I would discover that there was such a thing as post-abortion healing Bible studies, namely, *Surrendering the Secret.* This Bible study solidified my telling my truth, and that trusting God's truth transforms us all. Now, as a leader of this study, I call *Surrendering the Secret* a "trust journey" through God's Word over the soul wound of abortion.

> We overcome by the blood of the Lamb and the word of our testimony! (Revelation 12:11).

I am overwhelmed that God has used the deepest shame of my life to demonstrate to me the true mercy of the cross and to ignite in me a passion to share the truth that surrendering to Him empowers and frees!

—Tricia Heflin,
Surrendering the Secret National Leader, Texas

The Daughter's Story

In just a few short weeks, my amazing hubby and I will be celebrating eight incredible years of life as *one!* What an insane, wild, fun, scary, exhilarating, *blessed* ride it has truly been! God has never abandoned us, not for one single second. He has faithfully carried us through amazing seasons as well as heartbreaking ones—through growth and hurt and confusion, to hope and exceedingly great joy and promise! He sure writes the best stories, doesn't He?

Shortly after Chris and I were married, God planned an incredible moment for my mom and me. It was a surprise encounter and an experience that would change both of us for the better. We were planning a girls' retreat together at a coffee shop just down the street from my house. We always have such a blast together, and this was no exception. As we dreamed and planned, however, I could not shake the sense that there was something blocking our conversation. I specifically felt the Lord leading me to ask her if there was something she needed to tell me.

"I had an abortion." Those four little words fell reluctantly out of the mouth of the last person I would have ever expected to hear them from. It's actually quite hard for me to even remember her being so afraid to speak those words out loud. The boldness she has now to tell any and everyone who will listen is truly remarkable and an absolute miracle! I know that telling me, her daughter, was perhaps one of the most difficult, but it was a crucial step toward her journey to freedom.

The enemy had convinced her that rejection would surely follow such a confession. However, nothing could be further from the truth. The truth always empowers and *frees* us! Not only did I feel immediate compassion and love for my mom, but I also felt a strange understanding come over me in regard to my own life. As the truth was setting her free, it also set me free.

All of a sudden, I began to make sense of so many of the things in my life that I could never understand before: why she felt the need to overprotect me from everything; my own struggles to stay pure; and countless other decisions she made in raising me, which had been guided by the guilt of her secret. Our relationship was strengthened as a result of her confession, because I finally knew that she wasn't as perfect as I had originally thought. She was capable of sin and in need of forgiveness, just like me. It was an incredible moment that God had planned for us, and a conversation I will treasure forever.

Since then, I have watched God redeem my mom's story and use it to set so many countless others free. Honestly, as a mother of three, I now feel the tragedy and heartbreak of abortion at a much deeper level. Falling in love with your children will do that to you. I understand her pain so much more, and I pray for God to use her story to save others from such a choice. Whatever place in life this finds you, may you know that you are never too far out of His reach. Love and grace are just a prayer away. *Freedom* awaits you. Life that is truly life (Jude 21) lies on the other side of surrender.

—Jenni,
A very proud daughter

"Mommy Had an Abortion"
By Kelly Clinger

Those are words I never thought I would say to my children. *In fact, I was never going to tell them.* I didn't want to explain what abortion was, much less tell them that their own mother had made such a terrible, sinful choice—twice.

When I was asked to be a spokesperson for the Silent No More Awareness Campaign, toward the end of 2010, they wanted to be sure that my immediate family knew my past before I began traveling the country talking about it. Of course, my husband knew most of the details (although more things surface as time goes on), *but how was I going to tell my kids that I killed two of their siblings?*

My daughter was 14 and my son was 8 at the time. I didn't want them to be disappointed in me. I didn't want them to hate me. *I didn't want them to feel about me the way I felt about myself.*

I sat the kids down on the couch and took a deep breath. I asked them if they knew what abortion was. My daughter said she had heard the word before but wasn't sure what it was. My son was clueless. As I began to explain it, the horror of it was all over their faces. "How could anyone do that?" my son asked. He kept asking questions, but my daughter's silence told me that she knew there was a reason I was talking to them about abortion.

I began to cry as I said, "Mommy had two abortions 10 years ago. You have two siblings in heaven."

I am crying now as I think about the shock and disappointment on their faces. It felt like the mommy they knew wasn't who they thought she was. I wonder about all of the questions that raced through their heads during those few seconds—all of the things they would be able to articulate years afterward but couldn't process in their young minds at that point.

My daughter scooted closer to me and threw her arms around me. "I forgive you, Mom. It's okay," she said. "I do too," my son said. "And when I get older, I'm *never* going to let my wife do that." We all cried together.

I went on to tell them about praying and asking God if the babies were boys or girls and what He would like me to name them. I told them about how God said they were both girls, and we had named them Goodness and Mercy. "Like the Bible verse!" my son shouted.

That was a few years ago, and they've heard Mommy talk about Goodness and Mercy a lot now. Anytime we hear a song with Psalm 23 in it, or someone reads that Scripture, my son will proudly announce, "Those are my sisters!"

Abortion is a common topic around our dinner table. I joined the fight for life by myself, but we now fight together as a family.

When Mother's Day approaches, many feel the sting of loss, but along with the sting, I feel the guilt. I will have two Mother's Day cards missing—my breakfast in bed will be prepared by two children instead of four. There is a void that will not be filled until I see Jesus face-to-face. But until then, my hope remains in this: "Surely goodness and mercy shall follow me all the days of my life" (Psalm 23:6).

From a Father's Heart: Men and Abortion

Not only does abortion hurt women, but it also hurts men. As more women respond to the healing journey of a past abortion, God is clearly stirring the hearts of men across the nation as well. At the national headquarters of Surrendering the Secret, calls come in on a regular basis seeking someone to talk to who understands the loss of fatherhood caused by abortion. Abortion is the antithesis of all that God created, called, equipped and empowered men to do and experience in life!

Men want to provide for and protect others, especially their women and children. Most men tend to fix things, stuff things and control things, yet they also want to succeed and accomplish things.

How do men deal and cope with abortion? Men experience many emotions and start acting out in multiple ways to deal with the pain, guilt, grief and inability to protect their child, including these ways:

- Stuffing feelings
- Drinking
- Anxiety
- Withdrawing
- No relationships
- Drugging
- Depression
- Cynicism
- Multiple unhealthy relationships
- No motivation to excel
- Feelings of failure
- Low self-worth
- Disdain for women

Men who originally agreed with or even pressed for abortion often bury their feelings and behavior by justifying their decision. Not so different from the rationalizations women use, here are a few common rationalizations:

- It was legal and best for everyone.
- We can't afford a child right now.
- Everybody has abortions; it's not a big deal.
- The timing wasn't right to get married.
- We hardly knew each other.

In most cases, it's not easy for men to join other men they don't know to pursue post-abortion recovery. It's difficult for men, at first, to open up about past behaviors or share feelings and thoughts and participate in a post-abortion group. It takes a great deal of courage and humility for a man to step into to a group setting and make himself vulnerable to others emotionally and spiritually.

When they do join a group, in a short period of time trust and bonding build, and honest dialogue in sharing feelings and emotions are expressed. Some men share more openly, easily and, at times, passionately, while others suppress their feelings, "fighting" instead of dealing with their pent-up emotions.

After a few weeks, tears appear, and deep personal feelings are shared instead of trying to avoid or fix others. Hardened hearts and offenses begin softening and evidence of the healing process can occur through the power of the Holy Spirit.

For some men, the healing is deeper and more profound earlier in the group process than for other men. God is at work transforming each of their hearts, filling these men with hope, wisdom and discernment, and bringing to the surface a repentant spirit and confession of sin. It is a life-changing experience to watch 1 John 1:9 come to life on the faces of these men:

> If we confess our sins, [God] is faithful and righteous to forgive us our sins and to cleanse us from all unrighteousness.

As trust, confidence and insight build, the men start questioning and confronting one another. In most cases, this is done lovingly and respectfully and is received very well. As they begin to operate as a team, building unity and praying for each other, the healing process takes place.

Conversation and interaction increase, stuffed memories and emotions are released, and detailed personal experiences and testimonies are shared.

Men don't like to fail or feel helpless, hopeless, trapped, out of control or feel like they have let others down, especially family, friends and an unborn child! When a man experiences an abortion he did not want to happen, everything inside him cries out, "Failure!" Since he wasn't able to save and protect his child, anger and resentment begin to build. Anger is caused by:

- Hurt
- Injustice
- Fear
- Offense
- Frustration
- Shame

When men take the time to complete each chapter of *Surrendering the Secret*, they are filled with Scripture, self-revealing questions and truth that sets them free from guilt and shame. Greater and deeper signs of healing and forgiveness are revealed to the point that the men are more transparent about other things in life and they experience God's love and grace. Transformation takes place in these men through the power of the Holy Spirit helping them to fulfill God's calling and destiny in their lives. In the end, they feel forgiven and empowered, and they experience the joy of the Lord!

Written with Sol Pitchon, MA
President and CEO New Life Solutions, St. Petersburg, Florida

Victims of Abortion: Baby, Mom *and* Dad

My paternal instincts began kicking in, but I didn't show it. In my heart, I wanted to somehow stop the procedure and save the baby. I felt so helpless. I rubbed and rubbed her stomach, thinking I could soothe the baby, or at least let it know it was loved, if just for a short time. I wanted to hold it. I wanted to hug it. I wanted it to live, like the baby chicks and rabbits I had nursed back to life as a child. I wanted to die in its place. Sadness overcame every muscle in my body. It was just so sad!

—Dan, post-abortion father

It is a simple fact that conception of a child requires the equal biological participation of a female and male—a mother and a father. The baby is obviously the first victim in abortion. The pro-life community has leaned toward spotlighting the mother as a victim, while often downplaying or even ignoring the fact that the baby's father is also a victim of the lies of a culture that advocates abortion.

The *Roe vs. Wade* Supreme Court decision of 1973 violently swung the door open for widespread legalized abortion in the U.S. The court focused on the woman's right to privacy while the personhood of the child in the womb was disregarded. So too were the rights of the father.

In the immediate years following this decision, 12 states adopted laws protecting the rights of men by requiring the husband's consent before his wife could follow through with an abortion. In 1976, the Supreme Court evaluated those state laws and deemed them inconsistent with the basis and decision of the *Roe vs. Wade* case, and therefore, unconstitutional.

Here we are, nearly 40 years later. Millions and millions of men have been affected by abortion. Many have knowingly participated in abortions through a wide range of approaches, from passivity to coercion. Many others were uninformed, deceived or may have fought unsuccessfully for the lives of their unborn children.

Catherine Coyle, Ph.D., has done extensive research on the subject of men who have been harmed by abortion. In her book *Men and Abortion: A Path to Healing*, published in 1999, a man called Dan recounts the inner turmoil he experienced in accompanying his future wife during an abortion (you read an excerpt above). Helplessness and confusion were two common themes expressed by the men interviewed in Coyle's research.

The state laws related to abortion disregard the father, thereby communicating that the father has no final influence or authority. Fathers are, therefore, denied the paternal instinct that motivates them to care for their families. One post-abortion father who now counsels post-abortion men wrote, "As I reflect on God's purpose and role for men (found in the Word), I see that because of my choice of participating in this offensive sin of killing my unborn child, I *quit* life. I taught myself to shortcut life in all decisions in the future (husband decisions, father decisions, job decisions, etc.)."

What makes things worse is that men are more likely than women to go forward in denial about the negative emotions that profoundly affect their lives. Vincent Rue, Ph.D., a forerunner in researching the effects of abortion on men, wrote, "Men do grieve following abortion, but they are more likely to deny their grief or internalize their feelings of loss rather than openly express them.... When men do express their grief, they try to do so in culturally prescribed 'masculine' ways, i.e. anger, aggressiveness, control."

Post-abortion men experience tendencies toward angry and violent behavior as well as an overall sense of lost manhood. Common consequences include broken relationships; sexual dysfunction; substance abuse; self-hatred; ever-increasing feelings of grief, guilt and depression; as well as dangerous and even suicidal behavior.

King David described the body's reaction to secret sin: "When I kept silent [about my sin], my bones became brittle from my groaning all day long" (Psalm 32:3). John's first epistle stresses the importance of confession: "If we say, 'We have no sin,' we are deceiving ourselves, and the truth is not in us. If we confess our sins, He is faithful and righteous to forgive us our sins and to cleanse us from all unrighteousness" (1 John 1:8-9). James 5:16 takes confession even further: "Therefore, confess your sins to one another and pray for one another, so that you may be healed."

One has to wonder what would happen if there was widespread confession of this sin that has ravaged the nation. What would happen if mighty warriors, expressing strength through weakness, stepped into the front lines, creating a massive wave of confession and repentance? How would marriages be affected in the here and now? How would this culture be affected as a whole? Would the hearts of the fathers be turned back to the children?

What if, rather than hiding the truth of past and present sexual impurity, confessions and repentance became an igniting fire in our churches? What about those men living in the fortress of a heart hardened by the deceitfulness of sin, self-justification and resentment? The shame, guilt and blame can be so deeply rooted that these wounded warriors more often than not need fellow soldiers and armor bearers to fight alongside them.

Perhaps the real question is, "What would happen if men fought back?" Not with weapons of the flesh, but as Paul wrote in 2 Corinthians 10:3-4 (*NASB*): "For though we walk in the flesh, we do not war according to the flesh, for the weapons of our warfare are not of the flesh, but divinely powerful for the destruction of fortresses."

If you are a post-abortion father, the following initial steps can move you out of darkness and into the fight:

1. Acknowledge your responsibility.
2. Confess to God and at least one other person you can trust.
3. Seek out available resources for post-abortion men, and follow through.

When a man struggles with sin, he is likely to keep his secret. However, biblical wisdom tells him not to give in to fear, pride and shame. Forgiveness and healing are achievable. Be a warrior; go after your victory!

Ann Reed, Writer and Friend of Surrendering the Secret
American Family Association, Tupelo, MS

This article is adapted from the full version available in the January 2013 edition of AFA Journal: http://www.afajournal.org/2013/January/012013abortion_dads.html (accessed April 2014). Used by permission.

The Men Impacted by Abortion

This collection is not intended to serve as an all-inclusive list, rather, an overview of possible scenarios and reactions that men might have to an abortion experience.

The father was adamantly opposed to the procedure.
This man may have an immediate and overwhelming response. It is hard for him to separate the feelings he is experiencing, but they include grief, guilt, rage/anger, and a sense of male impotence, i.e., he couldn't protect his partner or his child. He may be inclined to make repeated contact with his partner in an effort to understand how the decision was made.

**The father was opposed to the procedure
but did not go to extremes to prevent it.**
This man may also have an immediate reaction of sadness, grief and a sense of not being able to protect. He may experience anger, but not full-blown rage, as well as the other emotions listed above. He is not as prone to a violent reaction to his grief.

**The father first supported the abortion decision
and then changed his mind.**
This man holds himself responsible in a special way because he
agreed and then changed his mind. So the abortion progressed any-
way. This seems to happen more frequently within marriages. This
can become an issue within the relationship that interferes with basic
trust and with intimate couple relations.

The father appeared to be neutral on the issue.
This man supported the choice of the mother. Some men are actually
opposed, but society has urged him to be supportive of her decision.
Other men find the abortion decision to serve them well at a particular point in their lives.

The man who is unable to articulate how he really feels may react
like the first two groups of men. The man who is truly in agreement or
neutral in the abortion decision may not feel anything until years later.

**The father simply abandoned the woman
in the face of pregnancy.**
The man who abandoned the woman may not be troubled by the
event but may later find himself bothered by his behavior. This man
may have several abortion experiences.

**The father forced the abortion decision or threatened
to withdraw support if abortion was not chosen.**
The man who forces the abortion decision may have many abortion losses in a lifetime. Often, the relationship that resulted in the
abortion may no longer be active. The relationship may break apart
because the woman and the man react differently. The woman who
is forced into an abortion decision may have an immediate adverse
reaction that the man may not be able to understand. He may tell her
to "get over it" if she tries to speak of her confusion or discomfort.
This undercuts the relationship. Her discomfort might also bother
him and so the relationship might dissolve.

**The father was not told about the abortion
until after it occurred.**
This man may react with confusion because his partner did not dis-
cuss this matter with him but made a unilateral decision. It is possible that he might not find out until years later when a conversation

with an acquaintance may bring the unfolding of the story. He experiences many conflicting emotions, wrestling with the strength of their relationship and the lack of trust. There is often much ambivalence and confusion experienced in this setting.

The father not certain an abortion has occurred, but upon hearing the description of post-abortion aftermath in women, recognizes the symptoms in a former partner.
This man may wonder if there was a pregnancy that he was responsible for. He is unable to confirm that a pregnancy occurred. This can sometimes lead to many unanswered questions.

The man married a woman who had an abortion experience with someone else.
This man may be engulfed in the vortex of the woman's reaction to her previous abortion(s). He may or may not have been told about the experience of abortion. He may be confused by what is happening with his partner and may be very concerned about her.

The man who is not the sexual partner.
This man may have been aware of, or actively participated in, the decision to abort through a relationship with the mother or father who had the abortion. He may be a friend or a relative, such as a brother or father. Many emotions are experienced by these men.

> Adapted from "The Impact of Abortion on Men," *Reclaiming Fatherhood*, National Office of Post-Abortion Reconciliation and Healing, 2007. http://www.menandabortion. info/l0-aftermath.html (accessed April 2014). Used by permission.

A Man's Perspective

In an effort to adapt *Surrendering the Secret* to be used as a healing program for men, I asked several men who had shared their stories of past abortions with me to complete these questions as they related with each of the eight steps to healing (the 8 chapters of the book) found in *Surrendering the Secret*. Many men were willing to share their abortion heartbreak.

The following answers were provided by Tim Schultz, founder of Lifetime Pregnancy Help Center in Springfield, Illinois. Tim can be contacted at 217-523-0100 or info@lifetimephc.org.

Contact www.patlayton.net for additional resources for men and for couples.

Chapter 1: A Surrendered Life

Question 1: As a man, how do you handle memories of your past, especially things you are ashamed of or don't like to talk about?

Answer 1: Before I was healed of my abortion, I would never deal with the issue, even if I were ever in a conversation where abortion came up. For at least 9 of the 15 years, I kept my abortion a secret. I didn't talk about it at all, not to my wife, not to anyone. Then I had a rebirth in my relationship with Christ! Because of the revival in my life, I now had an attitude about abortion. Even though my wife and I were not completely healed and were still keeping our own secret, I remember feeling disgusted with the whole abortion scene. "The big nasty evil moneymaker that it is" was my only voice's opinion! The truth is, I was angry with myself! For more than six years we had kept our secret, and now that my spirit was awakened, I was angry. I was angry at me. I was angry at her. I was angry at the whole world.

When my wife received healing on a ministry retreat weekend, our lives changed *forever*! She came home and told me she was healed and had to tell everyone what the Lord had done for her, and it meant telling the secret! At that point, I was a little taken aback but I could not deny that I had a whole wife. She came home from that weekend better in every way. She was healed, at peace and armed with purpose. With a passion for my wife like never before, I knew that what I had stolen from her those 15 years before had been restored and made better than new. I wanted that for myself as well.

Question 2: Read the story of Abraham/Sarah and Hagar in Genesis 16:7-15 and share some thoughts of how Abraham handled this situation and how he might have felt about Hagar's suffering.

Answer 2: I'm not sure if Abraham was taking responsibility or not. Kind of looks like not—he threw the burden of decision right back to Sarah, telling her to "do with her what you will." Like a lot of men, I surrendered my decision to someone else. I placed the burden on my wife. I let someone else dictate my life, and that someone was not God. It was not even me. I was more worried about what people would think and say and about pleasing them than I was about pleasing the God who had blessed me with a new life. Like Abraham, I took matters into my own hands, or rather *didn't* take the responsibility for my actions I needed to take, and I made a mess of things.

Question 3: To this point in life, how have you dealt with the story of your aborted child or children, the woman involved, and your part in the choice? Is your story public? Who knows? How have you shared your story?

Answer 3: At this point in my life, my wife and I have embraced our abortion story together. We share the whole truth of our abortion so that others might make a better choice or be healed from a bad one. We also feel that God wants us to share that abortion is not the unforgivable sin. God does not hate us; He loves us. He's not mad at us; He wants us to share the truth about abortion on His behalf. We tell others, old and young, that an unplanned pregnancy is not a death sentence. My wife and I have now been married for more than 23 years and we thank God that through Him, we beat the odds! She has forgiven me for my part in the abortion. Through working together and following the path of *Surrendering the Secret,* the purity and trust I stole from her have been restored. Our story is very public. We are the founders and she is the director of Lifetime Pregnancy Help Center in Springfield, Illinois. Our lives are dedicated to saving women, babies and men from the heartbreak of abortion. We started by telling our five children, our parents and our families. I was a senior associate pastor at a local church when my wife received her healing. We asked the senior pastor if we could share her testimony with our entire congregation. Afterward, men and women filled the altar to ask questions and receive prayer for their own past abortions. That was the beginning of a new ministry God had for us. Now we share our story every day and thank God for every opportunity.

Your Response:

_____
_____
_____
_____
_____
_____
_____
_____
_____

Chapter 2: Sharing the Secret: Going Backward to Move Forward

Question 1: What were your life circumstances and relationships like at the time of your abortion?

Answer 1: I was 20 years old and living with my family out of state. My fiancée came to spend the summer and live with me before she went off to enjoy a full college basketball scholarship. We were both working and living a nice life with no cares to speak of. Everything was just as we had planned. Until we discovered she was pregnant.

Question 2: Was there anyone in your life you felt you could completely trust?

Answer 2: As I look back on it now, the only two people we told about the pregnancy were people I believed at the time we could trust. It turned out that the advice we received was not good. The influence to get an abortion was the order of the day.

Question 3: When or how did the idea of abortion come to mind? What other options did you consider?

Answer 3: Our first thoughts about abortion came through the advice of our friends. It all sounded logical and legitimate at the time. "This baby doesn't fit in the plan for your life right now!" "You can't have a baby; you will lose your $50,000 full-ride scholarship!" "It's just not time right now; you have your whole life ahead of you!" Unfortunately, we did not consider any other options; we just did our best to hide the pregnancy and get the abortion behind us. Our plan was to get it over with as soon as possible and move on with the plan we had for our life.

Question 4: How would you describe your abortion experience?

Answer 4: From what I can remember, it was a long, quiet ride as I tried to comfort my fiancée and just be there for support. Somehow, even then, I knew deep down that I had broken her trust and wondered if things would or could ever be the same. I was just hoping that we could just move on with our lives and leave it all behind. My plan was to never think of it or deal with it again. I just wanted to do whatever I could to fix it. It didn't turn out that way, strangely enough. I just took all the anger and disappointment from my fiancée and carried it every day with a smile on my face. Deep in my heart I was ashamed, and I knew I had lost her trust.

Question 5: Share thoughts and feelings you recall before, during and after the abortion.

Answer 5: The first thing I remember was disbelief. That test had to be wrong. We had barely been together. During the process of finding out the test was true, I just kept thinking, *How could I fix this?* We can have an abortion and just move on with the plan for our lives. No one would ever know. After the abortion, I just felt relief. At the same time, I felt remorse knowing deep down I was not a real man because real men do not murder their children. I just tried to work and stay busy. So did she. Somehow, I knew that if I slowed down enough to think about it I would have to face what I had done to my fiancée and my baby. The funny thing is, I was not even sure *why* I was ashamed. This seemed to be the best decision for me *and* for her. This feeling of confusion lasted for the next 15 years.

Question 6: What about you changed the day of the abortion?

Answer 6: I knew deep in my heart I had wounded my future wife in such a way that only God could fix it, and I remember crying at night and asking Him to help me make it right and heal our relationship. Trust had been broken on many levels, and it took 15 years for it to be renewed. Now that we have God in our lives, we have a whole new marriage; but honestly, we still work on it to this day.

Your Response:

_____

_____

_____

_____

_____

_____

_____

_____

_____

Chapter 3: What Is the Truth?

Question 1: During the process of the abortion decision, was there ever a discussion about the development of the unborn child? About the abortion procedure? About the possible medical or emotional risk?

Answer 1: No. We never discussed any of these issues; we just set a date and went through the process of showing up, having the abortion and going home and never speaking of it again.

Question 2: What thoughts or feelings did you have regarding the procedure itself?

Answer 2: When she walked out of the abortion room, I knew she would never be the same again. My heart was broken and I tried to comfort her by doing anything she wanted. I was committed to never leaving her to deal with it by herself unless she wanted to.

Question 3: Do you feel that you were informed about abortion in any way prior to the experience? What was your knowledge?

Answer 3: No, we were totally uninformed. We treated it like any other visit to the doctor. The doctor always knows best, right? He is a professional and he has our best interests at heart. We later discovered that was not true at all. We walked in alone and we walked out alone.

Question 4: Do you feel that you have any symptoms of post-abortion stress in your life now? Or have you in the past?

Answer 4: Through this healing process and doing the hard work it takes to confront a mistake like this one, we have received total healing in Jesus' name! God saved our marriage. The first nine years of our married life together were filled with resentment, fear, regret, depression and no self-discipline. I tried to cover up what we had done by staying busy and by never giving myself any time to think about it.

Through this journey, God has shown us how badly this decision has affected our entire lives, but He has also shown us He is a forgiving and healing God and wants His sons and daughters healed and whole in Him.

Your Response:

_____

_____

_____

_____

_____

_____

_____

_____

_____

Chapter 4: Like Drinking Poison

Question 1: Did you experience feelings of anger before the abortion experience?

Answer 1: Yes, I was angry with myself that I had broken trust and had no self-control. I had been so stupid as to not protect my fiancée.

Question 2: Have you had such feelings since?

Answer 2: The healing process my wife and I experience uncovered a lot of unresolved anger. We had experienced many things in our marriage that were directly related to this decision. It was not always a pretty or easy process to walk through and face these kinds of reactions. Let's just say that during this anger session one fluffy pillow was lost to the world. I used it to catch the brunt of my pent-up emotions—a process our leader used in this session that really worked for me. It felt so good to get it out, and I was set free that day.

Question 3: As you listened to the women in the *Surrendering the Secret* DVD, how were you affected?

Answer 3: I have had many anger issues. Honestly, I am still angry today at the abortion industry, at the lies and the evil that it pours out in our communities and on our people. We call ourselves a cultured society, yet we kill the most innocent people in our world for a profit! As we study past cultures and see how they sacrificed children and people in general, we see that life hasn't changed all that much. We still murder the most innocent for a profit! This makes me very angry! At the same time, God has shown me how to use that emotion for good by serving through a local crisis pregnancy center and helping other men get healed from a past abortion. I am now fighting the fight God's way.

Your Response:

_____

_____

_____

_____

_____

_____

_____

_____

_____

_____

Chapter 5: Forgiveness: The Golden Key to Freedom

Question 1: Do you feel that there is anyone you need to forgive about your abortion experience? Tell about it.

Answer 1: Not today. By the grace of God, I have been able to forgive and move on with the call on my life to help end abortion.

Question 2: Does anyone need to forgive you?

Answer 2: The only person I have really felt concerned about receiving forgiveness from is my wife, and she and I are healed. We have surrendered this secret and have moved from remorse to results! We serve together to do all we can to be sure no other young couple goes through this choice alone and without true and factual information.

Question 3: Did listening to the video give you any new revelation about a woman's response to a man's part in the abortion choice?

Answer 3: I knew my part. I know the part of most men in this decision. Many of us are just as scared and just as confused as the woman. It broke my heart to hear the stories of the women in the video and to realize the heartbreak that is caused by abortion for everyone!

Question 4: Do you feel that God has forgiven you of your part, if you had one, in the abortion choice?

Answer 4: Yes, I know I am forgiven and have taken on the responsibility to help other post-abortive men receive forgiveness and total healing by confessing their part in the abortion choice.

Your Response:

_____
_____
_____
_____
_____
_____
_____
_____
_____
_____
_____
_____
_____
_____

Chapter 6: The Great Exchange

Question 1: Are you a Christian? How do you know? When did you experience a saving faith in Jesus Christ?

Answer 1: Yes, I am saved today with a true relationship with Jesus and the Father. But we were both "saved" at the time of our abortion, but we had little self-control. I'm a preacher's son and she was a good church girl who loved the Lord. Yet we still committed this sin. God's Word says *all* fall short of His glory. We understand that the love of Jesus covers all of our sin. We are forgiven, and now we are responsible to speak the truth in love in order to save others.

Question 2: Have you actually dealt with your abortion spiritually, one on one with Christ?

Answer 2: Yes, and I continue to be motivated by Him to help others deal with their abortion experience as a part of the call on my life. I love to serve others in this area because I feel a special understanding of how we make this life-stealing choice and how much God wants to restore us.

Your Response:

_____

_____

_____

_____

_____

_____

_____

_____

_____

_____

_____

Chapter 7: The Peace of Release

Question 1: Have you experienced the time of "release" surrender or "memorial" for your unborn child?

Answer 1: Yes, it was very humbling and rewarding. To weep over my lost child and to be cleansed by tears of repentance changed my life and gave me new purpose. I now see people who have walked this journey through the Holy Spirit and allow God's power to move mountains of shame and loss out of the lives of people who are hurting.

Question 2: If you were to write a letter to your unborn child, what would you say to him or her? How would you say good-bye?

Answer 2: I would say I am sorry for not being a man, a father and a leader. I am sorry for being more concerned with being a man-pleaser than a God-pleaser. I am sorry for not protecting his mother and him. And I would ask for forgiveness and let him know that now, because of him, his mother and I have dedicated the rest of our lives to saving babies and helping people heal from this mistake. I would tell him that his life has left a legacy that helps us make sure that no one God places *in our path* has to be uneducated about abortion ever again.

Your Response:

_____

_____

_____

_____

_____

_____

_____

_____

_____

Chapter 8: Passing It On!

Question 1: Have you spoken out about abortion publicly? How? When? Where?

Answer 1: Yes, we have opened a Pregnancy Help Center in Illinois. We help people who are facing the choice for abortion every day. We share our story at churches and events and lead men and women through the healing process found in this book.

Question 2: How do you participate in sharing the truth about abortion with those you love and influence today?

Answer 2: I love to talk to people about the truth about abortion and help them see that an unplanned pregnancy is not some kind of death sentence! It is not the unforgivable sin. God always sees, always knows and always is there to rescue us from our mistakes. I love people right where they are and see them through the process of seeking and receiving forgiveness and healing. We tell them our story and show them what God has done for us and that He wants to do the same for them.

Question 3: What role do you feel men have in the freedom of abortion?

Answer 3: We have sacrificed a generation of innocent children on the altar of selfishness and the mighty dollar. Greed and selfishness have turned men, even men in our churches, away from God's plan for life. The blood of the unborn is on our hands and we will be held accountable. It is time for both men and women to seek healing and share the truth about abortion. It is time for us to take a stand, not through political rhetoric but through the Word of God. We must speak through love and restoration, but we must speak.

Question 4: How do you feel men's rights, as fathers, should be protected?

Answer 4: I believe that every man should have the right to know if he is the father of an unborn child. He should be given the opportunity to do the right thing. Even if the woman does not want the child, the man should be given the opportunity to keep his child. Give him the chance to support the woman throughout the pregnancy financially, spiritually and emotionally—whatever she needs. I believe the father, equally with the mother, should have the opportunity to choose life.

What will you *do to make a difference:*

_____
_____
_____
_____
_____
_____
_____
_____
_____
_____
_____
_____

My Advice Regarding Men and Abortion

The bottom line is that men need to find healing from abortion as much as women do, but they will process their feelings and their healing very differently.

For those women, family members or friends who have experienced an abortion and desire to share this journey with a man, here are a few ideas:

1. Be certain that *you* are healed first. I had a mentor many years ago who shared these wise words with me: "You can't give away what you do not have." Go through the

healing process found in this book and the partnering Bible study *Surrendering the Secret* with a friend, coach or Christian counselor. Be healed of your own pain, anger and loss before trying to help others.

2. Transparently share your own personal journey or experience. We always advise that the healing journey of abortion be shared with someone you trust. Maybe by sharing your own process without having any expectations of the other person, God will begin His work in that person's heart.

3. Contact the Surrendering the Secret International headquarters by email or through our website for information regarding men's resources, healing retreats and couples' healing.

4. Remember, you are not the healer. God is in charge and can handle the healing journey of your relative, spouse or friend. Join Him in the healing process through prayer, patience and your own surrender.

Couples and Abortion

Statistics indicate that it is a rare occurrence for a couple to survive an abortion decision. By the grace of God, some do, including my husband, Mike, and me. Our healing journey through an abortion was a long and tender one. God has brought us a long way as we have now celebrated 37 years of marriage and have served together in this ministry for close to 30 of those years. The work of healing through such a painful choice as abortion is certainly not an easy one—but God! His promises sustain us and His healing love allows us to see our failures as small compared to His power and plans.

Trust Him to lead your journey.

I pray that these stories of redemption encourage you.

Jen and Anthony

Anthony: Nine years after our abortion, I saw an announcement in our church's bulletin about *Surrendering the Secret*. I wanted to talk to Jen about it, but I didn't know how to bring it up. It was something we'd hidden, even from each other, for almost a decade.

Jen: After I registered, I knew I'd have to tell Anthony, mostly because I'd need him to watch our kids so I could go. I was really afraid to talk to him about it. I wasn't scared of his reaction; it was a fear of saying "abortion" out loud, of admitting that we'd had one, but, mostly, I needed help to heal from its devastation. That's how much of a secret I had let it become. I couldn't even say the word to my husband.

Anthony: I remember when she told me she was going to the STS study; I felt relieved, even glad. We sat in the car, at a stop sign, and I asked Jen if I could come too.

Jen: He held my hand when he asked. That was the first time we had ever talked about the abortion. Anthony's words really started to make this a safe discussion to have. It let me know that Anthony was hurting from our abortion too. That was something I'd never considered before, the fact that our abortion had wounded Anthony as well.

Anthony: As Jen went through the study, we would talk about the different steps she was on. In the beginning, that was key: talking about this event that had preceded our marriage and this secret that was really the foundation on which our marriage was based. I began to see, as she moved through the process, that I also needed healing; and so did our marriage.

Jen: Anthony's support and prayers not only carried me through the study but also gave me the freedom to really deal with the devastation our abortion caused. I began to see the damage our abortion had inflicted on our marriage. We both discovered that we were harboring deep resentment and unforgiveness toward one another.

Anthony: That bitterness affected how we lived as a couple. I often felt distant from Jen and would emotionally separate myself from her. I didn't see her as a safe person to talk to; and this led me to keep secrets from her.

Jen: Every day since our abortion, I felt that Anthony was running away from me emotionally, in actual geographic distance and spiritually. Even after we got married, I never felt completely connected to him. There was a real chasm between us, and I kept trying to cross it and reach him; but I never could. That lack of oneness created deep bitterness in me. Eventually, I wound up pushing Anthony away so this emotional separation would hurt less.

Anthony: As Jen and then I uncovered the root of these feelings, through STS, we were able to really face them and deal with them. We were able to recognize our anger and let it go in exchange for grace.

Jen: We were able to see our unforgiveness toward each other, and with Christ's help, we could extend forgiveness to each other. These experiences let us connect emotionally and spiritually in a way and with a depth that had never been a reality for us before.

Anthony: And we were finally able to grieve the loss of our child. Together. As parents. I was emotionally weak during the grieving process and was able to lean on Jen for strength and encouragement. This was a point of genuine growth in our marriage for us to be able to be there and show our love and support for one another.

Jen: Through STS, we found grace for ourselves and for each other. We forgave one another and let go of years of bitterness. We had a unity in our marriage that had not existed before; we even started dreaming about doing ministry together! Through this study, God enabled us to come together as a couple and build a new foundation for our broken marriage based on truth, transparency, trust and, above all, the grace of Jesus Christ.

Tricia and Steve

By the time I was leading *Surrendering the Secret* classes, I had begun to share publicly that abortion was true of me, and I shared about the healing power of God's Word. I had told my story of abortion to our children and most family members. While my husband, Steve, was not exactly thrilled, he was okay with it.

God had done such a healing work in my life through *Surrendering the Secret*, I felt free! Free in a way I'd never understood before—free from guilt and shame. Forgiven. Cleansed. Redeemed!

The experience of telling the *truth*, surrendering the *secret* of abortion and exposing it to God's light of truth created in me a freedom I couldn't keep to myself. While I was able to share with many other women, I so longed for my husband and me to be in this together. We'd certainly chosen abortion together, but also together, we had hidden this secret for more than 25 years. *Hidden* was still a comfortable place for Steve. He seemed fine with letting it be *my issue* and now, it seemed, fine with letting it be *my healing*.

Each heart knows its own bitterness, and no one else can share its joy (Proverbs 14:10, *NIV*).

The first time I heard this Bible verse, I thought, *That's it! Steve will never truly understand what I went through and what pain I feel in my heart over the abortion*. While I took comfort in that verse, trusting that God understood and even inspired this verse that helped me, I longed for Steve to *get it*, at least a little.

I had led *Surrendering the Secret* Bible study groups for three years, volunteered as a counselor at a crisis pregnancy center and spoke whenever possible about this healing journey, and Steve couldn't help but notice the changes in his wife. To mention a few: confidence, kindness, increased faith, joy, closer relationship with our children and their support of this ministry. But every time I asked, "Will you do this study with me?" He would answer, "No!" "Will you watch the videos?" "No! Men don't like to talk about it" was his explanation. I kept praying and trusting.

One day, I received an email announcement that *Surrendering the Secret* was being offered as an online couples' study! We would meet via Skype each week. Another married couple with abortion in their past would be leading it. I forwarded the message to Steve. No!

A few weeks went by. I prayed and re-sent the message with a few added words from my own heart. He came in from work that day and said, "I got your message. And okay! Yes! I believe God is telling me to do this study with you."

Thank You, God! ☺ We started the next week!

One of the first questions asked of us was, "What led you to this study?" Steve said that for the past three years, he had watched me lead class after class and come home "on cloud nine" about women changing and what God was doing in their lives. He heard the Word of God practically pour out of me. He saw changes in me and in others like he'd never seen from the many other Bible studies I'd taught, or the Bible studies he and I had taught together. "Abortion was indeed our choice *together* and it was time he said yes to me instead of no!" Steve's hope was that we would grow closer through this study. That happened, yes, but also, Steve began to see that God knows and cares about every detail of our lives and that trust in His Word changes us and brings new freedom.

As we began the study, Steve said, "This is a woman's study!" God gave him a new perspective on what it's like for women to read the Bible: Even though most of the verses are written to "he" and about "him," not "her," women still have no doubt the Bible was written for them as well as for men!

Week Two: Steve said, "Abortion story? I don't have an abortion story." But as he worked through the pages of the study, Steve realized that he, too, had an abortion story, not just me. He remembered the events, the clinic, the feelings and even thoughts he'd had so long ago. He wrote, "I remember the long drive home thinking, *This is it between us. Look at what a horrible thing we have done together.*"

We didn't want to shame our families. His dad was a pastor, mine a deacon; we were Christians.

As we studied, we began to see the damage that abortion had done to us *both*, and that hiding and stuffing and never talking about it was *the* major factor in our relationship difficulties. We had separated and almost divorced 20-plus years earlier. The abortion had come up in counseling, but no counselor ever tagged it as a problem or even something we needed to resolve.

As we continued in the *Surrendering the Secret* study, Steve shared that he had asked God's forgiveness for the abortion hundreds of times over the years. He had never asked for mine. We have now forgiven each other for this grievous act and regretted mistake. We now live in the truth of God's forgiveness!

Steve said, and I agree, that the most meaningful part of the study, *if* we had to choose one, was the memorial time. The peace of release! Writing a letter to his child was difficult for Steve, but freeing. It allowed grief.

> Dear Son (we believe God revealed we had a son), I'm sorry *is not enough*! We snuffed you out before you had a chance. I'm sorry. I love you and long to see you. —DAD!

I left planning the memorial up to Steve. He said to bring the letters we'd written to our unborn child. Letters, books and Bible in tow, we got in the car. First stop was the grocery store. I was choosing a flower and here came Steve holding a balloon. I remember thinking that no one in the store had a clue why he was carrying this blue balloon. No one but me. It felt like it was just God and us. Back in the car, I really had no idea where we were going, maybe a pretty hilltop or a park?

Steve turned into a beautiful cemetery. I gulped, but trusted.

> Even though I walk through the valley of the shadow of death, I fear no evil, for You are with me; Your rod and Your staff, they comfort me (Psalm 23:4, *NASB*).

We read our letters and cried together, allowing ourselves for the first time ever to express our grief for this child. "This should have never happened. I miss him. I wish we'd known him." Steve released the balloon. Picked up by the wind, it headed straight for a group of trees. Clasping hands, we held our collective breath for a second as we watched that little blue circle bounce its way through a perfect archway of branches. We watched until its heavenward dance could no longer be seen. Closure. God is so good!

We know that God has more for us, and He has healed us. Steve wrote in his book, and we both trust as stated in Joel 2:25, that God will continue to restore the years that were lost through shame and guilt and fear. We trust that God wants us to live for greater things than ourselves, to serve others and to realize that His power is revealed in our weakness!

I asked Steve, "Would you recommend that couples who have chosen abortion together do this study?" Yes! "Highly recommend?" Yes! ☺

Glenn and Jean: A Man's Story About the Impact of Abortion on His Marriage

My name is Glenn Chennault, and I am 68 years old. I am a father of an aborted child. It has taken 42 years for me to be able to share my story with anyone. This is my story.

On February 19, 1967, I married my high school and college sweetheart, Jean Moody. Jean graduated from college to be an elementary school teacher. We were living in a small town in Mississippi, where Jean was teaching and I was working for a metal building manufacturer.

Life was good.

In the later part of that year, we found out that Jean had been exposed to German measles. She was soon diagnosed with the disease. Then we came to know that she was pregnant with what would have been our first child. After the doctor examined Jean and explained to us all the things that could be wrong with our baby, he recommended that for Jean's health, we should have a "therapeutic abortion." What a technical word to add to the front of the word "abortion"! In the late 1960s abortions were not legal by law. The doctor said nothing of the long-term side effects this action was going to have on Jean and me.

We were both saved at an early age and were in church all of our lives. For guidance in the decision, we called on our pastor. Instead of his praying for healing, his advice was for us to do what the doctor said and to have the abortion. We did not find out until later that our pastor believed that life did not begin until the baby breathed on its own.

Many years passed, and I would not talk to Jean or friends about the abortion. I tried to block out of my mind that when I signed that consent form, I gave the doctor permission to kill my baby. For years I would reason it out by what the doctor told me when he came out of the operating room. He said that Jean had already started dilating and that she would have probably had a miscarriage. Because of this, I thought everything was okay.

One morning Jean woke me up and told me she had a dream where she saw our baby wrapped in white in the arms of Jesus. She knew our baby was safe in heaven. Even with this thought in mind, I still did not want to talk to anyone about the abortion or admit that there was anything wrong with me.

When abortion became legal, more and more people talked openly about it. Every time I heard the word, all I could think about was, how does this make Jean feel? It was eating me up inside all the time. When I did speak to a friend about our first child, I would always say that we lost our first child by a therapeutic abortion—always putting emphasis on *lost* and *therapeutic*.

Every year around the time of the abortion, Jean would start showing signs of depression. But I, being a workaholic, tried to never think about it. I thought, *I am a man. I can get through this all by myself!*

A couple of years ago, Jean talked about going to a Sanctity of Human Life service at our church. I remember telling her that if they started showing graphic pictures or describing what happens to a baby when aborted, I wanted her to get up and leave; she didn't need that! Yet, through that special service, Jean signed up and went through a small-group Bible study on abortion recovery called *Surrendering the Secret.* The change in Jean's life was something to watch! She began to urge me to do a men's study on abortion recovery. I thought, *Who thinks about men needing this type of study?* It has come to my understanding of reality that men hurt, as well.

I went through a study, and one particular Scripture spoke to me. It is found in James 5:16: "Therefore confess your sins to one another and pray for one another, so that you may be healed."

I found God's grace, mercy and forgiveness! I now know that my child is not lost but *is* in the arms of our loving Lord and Savior, Jesus Christ. Through His strength, I can live every day knowing He has forgiven me.

The Scriptures tell us that He allows us to go through deep valleys and that He is with us and will strengthen us to go out on the other side. We are to use those experiences to help others. Jean and I are doing just that in speaking opportunities and leading small-group studies to teach others, speaking the truth in love, of the effects of abortion. Through the study *Surrendering the Secret,* my prayer is that whoever reads my story will come to know they too can have the peace I have found. The secret lies in turning everything over to Jesus.

Other Family Members Involved in Abortion: A Letter from a Grandfather

Dear Steven and Paul,

I have often thought of what it would have been like to have you as my grandsons while I am still living on this earth God created for us. I was not fortunate enough to have a son of my own to do all the things guys enjoy doing together. We would have experienced many things together, like snow and water skiing, golf, tennis, fishing, football and basketball. It would have been great fun to fly RC planes together. You would have taught me a few tricks, I am sure.

You are grown young men now, raised by our heavenly Father. I am certain He has taken good care of you and these things we do in our brief time here on earth pale in comparison to our eternal experience.

Your mother was very young and afraid when you both came along. Although I cannot speak for her, I know she would have been a loving and caring mother. I take comfort in knowing the way of our Lord, and that you will welcome her with open arms when she comes to be with you in heaven. I believe her heart breaks for the loss of you not being with her here on earth.

Please ask our Lord to comfort her and give her peace.

With the love of your grandfather and grandmother and your mother, we will see you soon and forevermore.

Your Grandfather

About the Author

Pat's most precious role is being "Honey" (aka wife of 37 years) to Mike, mom to three amazing adults, mother-in-law to two beautiful women and "G" to five *perfect* grandchildren. Pat is a busy national speaker, author and life coach. She writes articles for newspapers, blogs, newsletters and ministry media, including Lifeway and Focus on the Family, and she serves as a member of the board of directors of Proverbs 31 Ministries.

Pat is the founder and president of an international ministry based in Tampa, Florida, that has become one of the nation's largest sanctity of life ministries. She has also spearheaded the founding of a crisis pregnancy intervention program (A Woman's Place); an adoption agency; a counseling and support ministry for families faced with life-threatening medical conditions of a preborn child; and Surrendering the Secret, an international post-abortion recovery ministry.

Pat's healing program for Surrendering the Secret was published in 2008, and it includes a leader's guide and DVD series. The ministry headquarters are located in Tampa, Florida. Through her national leadership staff and 1,700 international partners and churches, the ministry provides ministry support groups for men, women and couples all over the world.

Pat's latest and "most exciting ever" endeavor has been the founding of a National Women's Conference called "Imagine Me... Set Free." Her conferences take place throughout the year (schedule can be found at www.patlayton.net).

Pat shares her daily life—both the messes and the ministry— through her website and blog at www.patlayton.net.

Watch for Pat's upcoming book, *Life Unstuck*.

Also by Patricia K. Layton

coming soon from

PATRICIA K. LAYTON

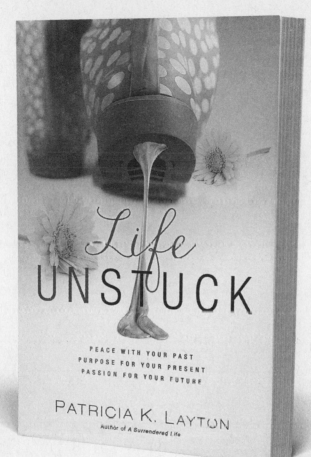

LIFE UNSTUCK

Peace with your past
Purpose for your present
Passion for your future

Life Unstuck
Patricia K. Layton
ISBN 978.08007.26386

This book offers hope for the woman who secretly suspects there is nothing more, but desperately dreams that there is . . .

Available wherever books are sold!